STRATEGIES
FOR TEACHING
High School Chorus

MENC wishes to thank
Carolynn A. Lindeman for developing and coordinating this series;
Randal Swiggum
for selecting, writing, and editing the strategies for this book;
Marcia MacCagno Neel for special editorial assistance;
and the following teachers for submitting strategies:

Jacqueline Blake

Steven O. Boehlke

Thomas Bromley

J. Bryan Burton

Jo-Ann L. Decker-St. Pierre

Christopher Dietz

Lawrence Doebler

Lauretta Graetz

Joe W. Grant

Jennifer Hillbrick

Dennis A. Jewett

Jeanne Julseth-Heinrich

Richard A. Larson

Shirley Letcher

Marcia MacCagno Neel

Patricia O'Toole

Melissa E. Popovich

Judy Sagen

Will Schmid

Rebecca R. Winnie

STRATEGIES
FOR TEACHING

High School Chorus

Compiled and edited by
Randal Swiggum

YOUR KEY TO
IMPLEMENTING
THE NATIONAL
STANDARDS
FOR MUSIC
EDUCATION

MUSIC EDUCATORS NATIONAL CONFERENCE

Series Editor: Carolynn A. Lindeman

Project Administrator: Margaret A. Senko

CONTENTS

57 total strategies

PREFACE

The Music Educators National Conference (MENC) created the
Strategies for Teaching series to help preservice and in-service music
educators implement the K–12 National Standards for Music
Education and the MENC Prekindergarten Standards. To address the
many components of the school music curriculum, each book in the
series focuses on a specific curricular area and a particular level. The
result is eleven books spanning the K–12 areas of band, chorus, general music, strings/orchestra, guitar, keyboard, and specialized ensembles. A prekindergarten book and a guide for college music methods
classes complete the series.

The purpose of the series is to seize the opportunity presented by the
landmark education legislation of 1994. With the passage of the
Goals 2000: Educate America Act, the arts were established for the
first time in our country's history as a core, challenging subject in
which all students need to demonstrate competence. Voluntary acad-
emic standards were called for in all nine of the identified core subjects—standards specifying what students need to know and be able
to do when they exit grades 4, 8, and 12.

In music, content and achievement standards were drafted by an
MENC task force. They were examined and commented on by music
teachers across the country, and the task force reviewed their comments and refined the standards. While all students in grades K–8 are
expected to meet the achievement standards specified for those levels,
two levels of achievement—proficient and advanced—are designated
for students in grades 9–12. Students who elect music courses for one
to two years beyond grade 8 are expected to perform at the proficient
level. Students who elect music courses for three to four years beyond
grade 8 are expected to perform at the advanced level.

The music standards, together with the dance, theatre, and visual arts
standards, were presented in final form—*National Standards for Arts
Education*—to the U.S. Secretary of Education in March 1994.
Recognizing the importance of early childhood education, MENC
went beyond the K–12 standards and established content and
achievement standards for the prekindergarten level as well, which are
included in MENC's *The School Music Program: A New Vision*.

Now the challenge at hand is to implement the standards at the state
and local levels. Implementation may require schools to expand the

resources necessary to achieve the standards as specified in MENC's *Opportunity-to-Learn Standards for Music Instruction: Grades PreK–12.* Teachers will need to examine their curricula to determine if they lead to achievement of the standards. For many, the standards reflect exactly what has always been included in the school music curriculum—they represent best practice. For others, the standards may call for some curricular expansion.

To assist in the implementation process, this series offers teaching strategies illustrating how the music standards can be put into action in the music classroom. The strategies themselves do not suggest a curriculum. That, of course, is the responsibility of school districts and individual teachers. The strategies, however, are designed to help in curriculum development, lesson planning, and assessment of music learning.

The teaching strategies are based on the content and achievement standards specified in the *National Standards for Arts Education* (K–12) and *The School Music Program: A New Vision* (PreK–12). Although the strategies, like the standards, are designed primarily for four-year-olds, fourth graders, eighth graders, and high school seniors, many may be developmentally appropriate for students in other grades. Each strategy, a lesson appropriate for a portion of a class session or a complete class session, includes an objective (a clear statement of what the student will be able to do), a list of necessary materials, a description of what prior student learning and experiences are expected, a set of procedures, and the indicators of success. A follow-up section identifies ways learning may be expanded.

The *Guide for Music Methods Classes* contains strategies appropriate for preservice instructional settings in choral, instrumental, and general music methods classes. The teaching strategies in this guide relate to the other books in the series and reflect a variety of teaching/learning styles.

Bringing a series of thirteen books from vision to reality required tremendous commitment from many, many music educators—not to mention the tireless help of the MENC publications staff. Literally hundreds of music teachers across the country answered the call to participate in this project, the largest such participation in an MENC publishing endeavor. The contributions of these teachers and the books' editors are proudly presented in the various publications.

—Carolynn A. Lindeman
Series Editor

Carolynn A. Lindeman, professor of music at San Francisco State University and president of the Music Educators National Conference (1996–1998), served on the MENC task force that developed the music education standards. She is the author of three college textbooks (The Musical Classroom, PianoLab, *and* MusicLab) *and numerous articles.*

INTRODUCTION

High school chorus students in Ottumwa, Iowa, were in for a surprise. Rehearsal had always been the same: an hour of singing. But today their director, Frances Elliott Clark, began rehearsal with a ten-minute discussion of music history. So what's so surprising about that? Well, it was 1896.

For more than one hundred years thoughtful music educators have recognized the interdependence of music performance and music knowledge. In 1972, a study by Charles Benner stated:

> "Performing group participation has little effect on musical behavior other than the acquisition of performance skills, unless there is a planned effort by the teacher to enrich the performing experience with additional kinds of musical understanding." (Charles Benner, *Teaching Performing Groups,* From Research to the Music Classroom, no. 2 [Reston: MENC, 1972] 10)

The National Standards for Music Education demonstrate the commitment of music educators to both performance skills and music knowledge. Even those standards that emphasize performance skills (1 and 2) imply performing with understanding. The standards that emphasize creating (3–5) show the interdependence of performance and knowledge of theory and style. And the standards that emphasize describing (6–9) focus on the importance of an integrated understanding of the whole picture of music in the world, as well as the ability to talk about it. A tall order for music educators indeed!

The intent of this book is to suggest teaching strategies that show the standards in action, giving students a variety of learning activities that go beyond performance skills only. Some strategies may prompt a "Hey, I already do that!" while others can be tried immediately "as is" or be adapted further. Some may spark a new strategy idea.

A typical choral rehearsal is rarely one activity, but actually a series of short rehearsals that call for a variety of approaches. The strategies vary from ideas for introducing a skill in a portion of a class session to plans for an entire class session. Some contain challenges that could be spread over several rehearsals or even weeks. The strategies generally focus on one objective, but they can and often do include other related learnings along the way.

Several strategies focus on the same piece of music in order to give examples of the diversity of learnings possible from a single choral work of quality. Much of the music used in the strategies is regarded as standard repertoire, and many of the more recent materials, including pieces reflecting various cultures, have already been shown to be worthy of classic status.

The strategies demonstrate a wide variety of learning styles (i.e., visual, aural, kinesthetic, verbal, and abstract). A number of them combine several learning styles at once, giving all students a chance to grasp a new or difficult idea as confidently as possible.

Under the heading Materials in the strategies, piano is not listed. It is assumed that the choral rehearsal room will be equipped with either a piano or another appropriate keyboard instrument for accompanying students' singing. Specific instruments needed for particular strategies are listed, however. Also, it is assumed that students will bring pencils to choral rehearsals. Always encourage students to use pencils in rehearsals to mark reminders and hints for reading their music.

Here are some suggestions for using this book:

- Begin to look at every choral octavo as a textbook full of learning possibilities. This approach makes choosing the highest quality music essential because only music of depth, lasting value, and compositional integrity will offer the possibilities of multidimensional learning that the standards imply. When reviewing possible repertoire, ask yourself more than "How can we sing this piece beautifully?"—ask, "What can I teach with this piece?" Look for choral works that will help teach certain concepts and understandings and then begin planning to teach those understandings.

- Use these strategies as models to create your own. Push the limits of your imagination. The worst thing that can happen if a new idea does not work is that it simply doesn't work. When studying these strategies, try to apply them to your own repertoire and your own choir. When developing your own strategies, try to address all learning styles in some way.

- Don't be afraid to use discussion as a strategy, but make sure you have planned it carefully, even writing down the questions you will ask to guide the discussion most effectively. Students learn more from the questions we ask than from the answers we give, and well-crafted classroom questioning is an art. Classroom discussions can get "messy," especially when they are based on an abstract or thoughtful question, but these open-ended moments can be very effective—if students leave class without all the answers, they will keep thinking until the next day.

- Don't be alarmed if your choral rehearsal occasionally starts to feel like a general music classroom. If we remember that our job is *music education* and not just getting ready for the next performance, we will use whatever strategies work to broaden our students' understanding of the way music *works*. This often looks more like general music than the traditional "maestro-centered," autocratic rehearsal style of our past. In fact, general music teachers will definitely be at an advantage in understanding the National Standards—borrow their strategies to enrich your teaching.

- Most of all, don't be overwhelmed by what seems like too much to accomplish. If your chorus sings one less piece each concert, you will have more time to enrich the rehearsal with thoughtful activities that push deeper into the music you are rehearsing. And there is no question that the time spent helping students really understand the music they are singing—how the music is put together, what the composer was trying to say, how the music fits into a style period, what makes it work compositionally, what it is saying emotionally, how to decipher its notation—is time well spent. It is time that will later pay big dividends in knowledge and skills combined, and time that will make learning new music easier and certainly more enjoyable as a result of the increased level of understanding.

Compared to the traditional choral experience, this comprehensive approach can be a threatening new paradigm. It takes more planning and reflection on the part of the teacher. It requires new strategies and some creativity. It takes some emphasis off the product (the concert) and puts it squarely on the process, which has no neat limits and clear borders. But the rewards for students are rich ones. And of course, therein lie the richest rewards for teachers, as well.

STRATEGIES

STANDARD 1A

Singing, alone and with others, a varied repertoire of music: Students sing with expression and technical accuracy a large and varied repertoire of vocal literature with a level of difficulty of 4, on a scale of 1 to 6, including some songs performed from memory.

Objective

- Students will demonstrate understanding of the element of timbre, especially as it relates to bright versus dark vocal color, in expressive singing of a piece with a level of difficulty of 4.

Materials

- "Now Is the Month of Maying" by Thomas Morley (Boston: E. C. Schirmer), 1155, SATB, Level 4; or another Level 4 madrigal or choral selection that calls for a darker- or brighter-than-usual vocal color
- Chalkboard

Prior Knowledge and Experiences

- Students have been rehearsing the selected work.

Procedures

1. During the warm-up, teach the choir the following vocalise:

2. When students are comfortable with the vocalise and are making a good sound, tell them to sing it as if they were an adult church choir. After they do so, which should result in a darker, warmer sound, ask them to sing the vocalise as if they were a professional opera chorus. Continue inviting them to sing the vocalise in different ways—as if they were forty-five years old, a college choir, a children's choir, and so on.

3. Lead a brief discussion about the flexibility and variety of colors available to the human voice, using your own voice to demonstrate. Point out that the characteristic sound of an oboe is always the same, that a xylophone always sounds like a xylophone, and that even the violin, which can achieve subtle variations of color, cannot parallel the many possibilities for the voice. Write the word "timbre" on the chalkboard and explain to students that this is the musical word for "color," and it is the name of the element of music they have been using and discussing.

4. Have students brainstorm to create a list of words on the chalkboard to describe vocal colors (nasal, flutey, and so on). If no student suggests them, add "bright" and "dark" to the list.

5. Ask students to sing the vocalise again, first as if they were a children's choir and then as if they were a mature adult choir. Have them identify which tone color was brighter and why, and ask them which vowels are generally brighter and which are darker. Have students first try making the "ee" vowel darker and then try making the "oh" vowel brighter. Experiment with these vowels to assess students' understanding of bright versus dark and of how to produce the difference vocally.

(continued)

6. Tell students to imagine that "1" on a scale of 1 to 10 is very dark and "10" is very bright. Then have them sing the vocalise at "3," at "1," and at "10." Ask them how they think "5" should sound.

7. Ask students to decide what number on the scale would be the most appropriate timbre for the mood of "Now Is the Month of Maying," which they have been rehearsing, and to defend their choice. Have students sing the piece with the timbre chosen by a large number.

Indicators of Success

■ Students appropriately adjust the brightness or darkness of their tone in warm-ups and choral pieces.

■ Students make critical decisions about the appropriateness of a particular tone color for a specific choral selection they are singing.

Follow-up

■ In subsequent rehearsals, apply students' other choices from step 7 until they reach a consensus about the most appropriate timbre for "Now Is the Month of Maying."

■ Continue to use the 1–10 scale and terms such as "bright" and "dark" in warm-ups and rehearsals to remind students of available tone colors. Discuss the appropriate timbre for other works being rehearsed, helping students begin to connect the ideas of tone color and emotional expressivity.

STANDARD 1B

Singing, alone and with others, a varied repertoire of music: Students sing music written in four parts, with and without accompaniment.

Objective

■ Students will develop independence in unaccompanied singing in four or more parts, maintaining tonality against dissonance and demonstrating pitch memory.

Materials

■ None required

Prior Knowledge and Experiences

■ Students have begun to sing music in parts unaccompanied.

Procedures

1. During the warm-up, ask the choir to sing "America," or another familiar melody, at a moderate tempo and with a clear pulse. Encourage them to use good vocal technique and accurate intonation.

2. Split the choir into four groups and have students sing "America" as a canon at two measures. Emphasize the importance of good intonation even when the notes "clash."

3. When students can sing the canon successfully in four groups, split the choir further into seven groups, making the split so that no one is standing near anyone else singing his or her part. Then ask students to try singing "America" as a canon at one measure.

4. When students are singing confidently, warn them that you will stop and hold random beats. [*Note:* Choose chords to hold that are obviously very dissonant.] Their challenge will be to maintain their sense of tonality when you move on.

5. Have students sing "America" as a canon, stopping when you indicate and then continuing on. Help them discover that "America" was not written to be sung as a round and, therefore, extreme "clashes," called *dissonance,* are created in singing it as one. Explain to them that holding their parts against dissonance is an important aspect of part singing. Finally, have students sing the canon straight through in their seven parts.

Indicators of Success

■ Students sing "America" as a canon with four or more parts and good intonation.

■ Students identify dissonant sounds and use the term dissonance appropriately.

Follow-up

■ Help students discover what dissonance looks like in written notation (many notes, or notes very close together). Let them find dissonant moments, both aurally and visually, in the music they are rehearsing.

Singing, alone and with others, a varied repertoire of music: Students sing music written in four parts, with and without accompaniment.

Objective

- Students will gain independence in singing unaccompanied in four parts, tuning chords as needed.

Materials

- Chalkboard
- Manuscript paper

Prior Knowledge and Experiences

- Students have some experience in part singing.

Procedures

1. During the warm-up, ask students to sing a descending five-note scale—*sol-fa-mi-re-do*—and sustain *do*. Emphasize good vocal technique and intonation.

2. Have basses and altos repeat what they just sang, but ask tenors to sing *sol-fa-mi-fa-sol*, sustaining *sol;* and sopranos to sing *sol-fa-sol-fa-mi*, sustaining *mi*. Have everyone sustain the final chord until they are secure in intonation.

3. Have students repeat this drill at different pitch levels, telling them to listen carefully to each other to be sure they are in tune.

4. Ask students what they are creating when they sustain the final notes. Have them share their terms and definitions and help them clarify their understanding. Explain that a *triad* is a simple kind of *chord*, which falls under the musical element *harmony*. Help students to understand the difference between these terms and to use them correctly.

5. Help students discover what a triad looks like in notation. Emphasize the importance of the third in determining the look and sound of a chord. Have students practice notating triads on their manuscript paper. As you identify the top, middle, or bottom note by letter name, they notate the triad.

6. Have students sing their parts, from steps 2 and 3, on "bing" (like bells, sustaining the "ng") and concentrate on listening to and tuning the chord.

Indicators of Success

- Students sing triads in tune and identify them aurally and visually.

Follow-up

- Using the procedures outlined above, teach students the concept of major versus minor triads—the difference in their sound and their visual construction. Define the terms *root, third,* and *fifth.* Show students how to break down a four-part chord built on a triad in their scores to discover which part has the root, the third, and the fifth. Introduce the idea of chords that use more than three different notes.

Singing, alone and with others, a varied repertoire of music: *Students sing music written in four parts, with and without accompaniment.*

Objective

- Students will develop their inner ear, pitch memory, and intonation skills, gaining confidence in unaccompanied singing of music in four parts.

Materials

- Any four-part, mostly homophonic, choral piece

Prior Knowledge and Experiences

- Students have had some success in unaccompanied part singing.
- Students have been rehearsing the selected piece.

Procedures

1. In the selected four-part choral piece, choose a section that students can sing fairly securely a capella and review it with them by having them sing through it once or twice.

2. Ask students to sing the same section silently but with intense energy while you conduct. To assess how they are singing in their heads, stop and say, "What word were you singing when I said stop?" Repeat this process until students are comfortable and can do it successfully.

3. Repeat the same process, but this time ask students to sing silently for four measures and then sing audibly and sustain the first note of the fifth measure. Check their intonation, and repeat this step several times until they are successful.

4. Have students sing aloud, then silently, then aloud, and so on, through the whole piece. Encourage accurate intonation and rhythmic precision in both the silent and the sung phrases. Identify the stopping and starting places before beginning, or make it a concentration game by asking students to follow your signal for silent or audible as you continue to conduct.

5. Discuss with students the importance of inner-ear listening at all times. Explain that this kind of intense concentration is important whether they are singing or waiting to sing.

Indicators of Success

- Students sing, unaccompanied, a four-part choral piece accurately, in tune, and with rhythmic precision.

Follow-up

- Review the idea of pitch memory in subsequent rehearsals. Start rehearsals by having students try to sing the opening chord of a piece they have been rehearsing without giving them any starting pitches. Remind them to work on inner-ear listening, and check their progress by having them sing selected measures of familiar pieces inaudibly, focusing on intonation as well as pitch.

Singing, alone and with others, a varied repertoire of music: Students
demonstrate well-developed ensemble skills.

Objective

- Students will demonstrate rhythmic precision and sensitivity toward the conductor's gesture.

Materials

- Tennis ball

Prior Knowledge and Experiences

- Students can perform a selected piece from memory (optional; see step 3).

Procedures

1. Begin the warm-up with a concentration game, asking students to mirror your gestures exactly. Starting with your hands at your sides, raise your right hand quickly and mechanically from the elbow, keeping the upper arm still. Do the same thing with the left hand, while the right arm goes back to your side. Mix and match these "robotic" gestures, encouraging students to mirror you rather than follow you. Occasionally raise a full arm in a salute straight up. Create expected patterns of gesture that are interrupted by unexpected surprises, and vary the length of pauses between gestures. Keep the atmosphere light, but encourage intense, focused concentration.

2. During the breathing warm-up, ask students to hiss quarter notes. Show varying styles (legato and staccato) of quarter notes with your gestures, occasionally showing longer note values and fermatas. Encourage students to reflect your gestures exactly with regard to tempo and style.

3. Introduce the "I Can Lose You in One Measure" game. Using the hissing warm-up exercise, assorted vocalises, or actual repertoire, challenge students to follow you as you vary the tempo wildly. Set it up as a competition of sorts between you and the students, and reward them when their precision and accuracy warrant it.

4. To focus concentration on the initial attack of the phrase, give students pitches for a chord to sing on "tah." Toss a tennis ball straight up in front of you and ask them to sing their chord exactly as the ball hits your hand coming down.

5. When students are precise in singing with the landing of the tennis ball, invite a student to conduct the "tah" chord without any coaching. Introduce the term *upbeat,* and guide students, through trial and error, to discover the importance of the upbeat preparation in the gesture (remembering the tennis ball). Help them discover all the information contained in this one gesture (tempo, when to breathe, dynamics, and so on). Have students practice conducting upbeats and downbeats, with the choir responding to their gestures.

Indicators of Success

- Students attack phrases and follow the conductor's gestures with increasing rhythmic precision.

Follow-up

- Introduce the terms *ictus* and *rubato,* and teach students to use them correctly. Show students the basic conducting patterns of the music you are rehearsing, and then let them conduct themselves as they sing. Invite individuals to conduct the group.

STANDARD 1C

Singing, alone and with others, a varied repertoire of music: Students demonstrate well-developed ensemble skills.

Objective

- Students will perform legato phrases in slow tempos with rhythmic precision and assess their ensemble skills.

Materials

- Slow, legato work (e.g., "Sicut Cervus" by Giovanni Pierluigi Palestrina, any standard edition, Level 4)

Prior Knowledge and Experiences

- Students have been rehearsing the selected piece and are confident of the pitches and rhythms.

Procedures

1. Have students stand in choral formation and rest the heel of their right hand on the left shoulder of their neighbor to the right so that they can lightly tap their fingers on the neighbor's shoulders.

2. Set a tempo and then conduct students, having them practice tapping eighth notes and quarter notes with absolutely precise tempos. Alternate measures of each, encouraging students to be sensitive to slight variations in tempo.

3. Have students continue to tap as they sing sections of the selected piece. Have them do this in many variations: with and without a conductor, tapping various lengths of notes (eighths, quarters, or sixteenths, depending on the piece and its tempo), and tapping with their eyes closed. Always begin the tapping first to establish the tempo and enable students to settle into it.

4. Ask students to evaluate themselves, considering where they were not exactly together, where they may have been too fast or too slow, how they compared to those around them, and how they responded to your conducting. Make sure students evaluate their precision correctly.

5. Have students sing the piece a final time without tapping, but keeping the rhythm in their heads and concentrating on singing together.

Indicators of Success

- Students perform legato phrases in slow tempos with rhythmic precision and are sensitive to the ensemble.

Follow-up

- Have students tap subdivided eighth or sixteenth notes as they sing a piece with rubato to determine whether they can tap the notes with ensemble precision as you vary the tempo slightly.

Advanced

STANDARD 1D

Singing, alone and with others, a varied repertoire of music: Students sing with expression and technical accuracy a large and varied repertoire of vocal literature with a level of difficulty of 5, on a scale of 1 to 6.

Objective

- Students will sing a composition with a level of difficulty of 5 from their repertoire with heightened expression and intensity after exploring it dramatically.

Materials

- "Valiant for Truth" by Ralph Vaughan Williams (New York: Oxford University Press), 0-19353-529-7, SATB, Level 5, or another Level 5 choral work with a highly descriptive or narrative text, such as "Jesus Said to the Blind Man" by Melchior Vulpius, arr. Hans Eggebrecht (St. Louis: Concordia Publishing House), 981027, SATB; "I Love My Love," Cornish folk song, arr. Gustav Holst (New York: G. Schirmer/Hal Leonard Corporation), 5029920, SATB; "When David Heard" by Norman Dinerstein (New York: Boosey & Hawkes), BH 6014, SATB; or "When David Heard" by Thomas Weelkes (New York: Oxford University Press), 0-19352-211-X, SATB

Prior Knowledge and Experiences

- Students have just memorized the selected piece.

Procedures

1. Divide choir into three groups and assign each group a section of "Valiant for Truth" with a clear beginning and ending (first group, meas. 1–25; second group, meas. 26–41; and third group, meas. 42–end).

2. Give the groups about twenty minutes to create dramatizations of their sections of the work. Explain that everyone must be involved in the final performance and that the groups must use movement and mime only (no sounds). Encourage students not only to dramatize the story line of the text but to consider the underlying emotional content as well. [*Note:* If this activity will require more space than the choral classroom will allow, move to the auditorium stage or gymnasium.]

3. When the groups are ready, have each group perform its section of the work, in turn, while the other groups sing to accompany them. This should create a multidimensional classroom performance of considerable intensity.

4. After the entire work has been sung and dramatized without interruption, invite students to react to the experience by writing in their journals or portfolios.

5. Discuss the experience with students, asking what their favorite moment was and why, what moment worked effectively for them, where they saw an especially strong connection between what was happening in the music and how it was dramatized, and what new insights into the text they discovered. Help students focus on what aspects of this experience they can apply directly to their performance of the piece.

6. Have students sing through the piece without movement but with their newly developed sensitivity to expression.

Indicators of Success

- Students perform a piece with heightened expression and intensity.

Follow-up

- Use this strategy with a foreign-language piece the students are working on, encouraging them to explore and understand the meaning of a text in an unfamiliar language.

STANDARD 1E

Singing, alone and with others, a varied repertoire of music: Students sing music written in more than four parts.

Objective

- Students will experiment with texture and add parts to a four-part choral work.

Materials

- "David's Lamentation" by William Billings (Fort Lauderdale, FL: Walton Music Corporation), W2203, SATB, Level 2; or a similar early American partsong

Prior Knowledge and Experiences

- Students are confident singing unaccompanied in four parts.

- Students have been introduced to the element of texture.

- Students have rehearsed "David's Lamentation" in a previous class.

Procedures

1. Review with students the first section of "David's Lamentation" by asking who has the melody [the tenors] and how can they tell it is the melody. [It's the most interesting, most tuneful, and so on.] Then ask students why it is unusual for tenors to have the melody. [We usually think of the sopranos as carrying the melody in homophonic music.] Explain to students that early American composers such as Billings often placed the melody in the tenor part in these types of partsongs.

2. Have students offer suggestions on how to highlight or underline the melody more. Try various suggestions with the group.

3. If no student has already suggested it, try adding some sopranos to the tenor part. Move a group of sopranos to the tenor section, run a quick rehearsal of the tenor part, and then ask the entire choir to sing the first section of the piece. Emphasize the importance of listening, both to tune the octaves (between the tenors and sopranos who are all singing the tenor part) and to enjoy the new sounds being created. Ask students how many parts they are singing in now. [Five.] Then ask them what musical element they have changed. [Texture.] (If necessary, review with students a definition of thick and thin textures.)

4. Explain that the performance practice in Billings's day did indeed have tenors doubling the soprano part and vice versa. Ask students how to make the texture even thicker and try out some of their suggestions.

5. When students are familiar with the entire piece, ask them which sections of the piece they feel could use the six-part texture. Have them experiment with all the suggestions until they discover that the strictly homophonic sections work best (e.g., the opening section and the "O my son" section). Ask them what the effect of thickening the texture is and how it makes them feel.

Indicators of Success

- Students make effective decisions regarding texture and add parts to a four-part choral work.

Follow-up

■ Help students to see variations in texture in all of their repertoire. Discuss with students compositional choices from a composer's standpoint, helping them discover the composer's intent and the expressive impact of such variations.

STANDARD 1F

Singing, alone and with others, a varied repertoire of music: Students sing in small ensembles with one student on a part.

Objective

- Students will perform a madrigal accurately and expressively as part of a small ensemble with one student on a part.

Materials

- Four- or five-part madrigal— for example, "Fair Phyllis I Saw Sitting All Alone" by John Farmer (Fort Lauderdale, FL: Walton Music Corporation), W8000, SATB, Level 3; "Adieu, Ye City-Prisoning Towers" by Thomas Tomkins, SSATB, Level 3, in *Oxford Book of English Madrigals,* edited by Philip Ledger (New York: Oxford University Press, 1979); or "April Is in My Mistress' Face" by Thomas Morley (Boston: E. C. Schirmer), 1612, SATB, Level 3

Prior Knowledge and Experiences

- Students have sufficient experience to handle the selected madrigal in a large group with few technical difficulties.

Procedures

1. Rehearse the selected madrigal with the choir. At appropriate points, discuss with them relevant performance practices and characteristics of madrigal singing. Point out that madrigals were written for recreational singing by educated courtiers, that original scores were "partbooks" with only one singer's part to a book, and that the music was written in polyphonic style with each part having melodic material and equal importance.

2. Tell students to note other aspects of madrigal style, such as text-painting, dance-like rhythms, and expressive harmonies. Have students guess who sang the selected madrigal originally, where it was sung, and why. Ask students how many singers they think were on each part.

3. When students are confident of their parts, divide them into prearranged quartets (or double quartets if students are insecure). Tell students to practice in their quartets by standing in a semicircle to maintain eye contact and ensemble precision, to practice beginning and ending the piece together, and to evaluate their own performance and make adjustments.

4. Give each small ensemble the opportunity to perform for the class. If the piece is strophic, perhaps have one or more small ensembles sing, in turn, on verses. If there are "fa-la" refrains, use one or more small groups on the verses that precede them. Then ask students whether one voice on a part or many voices on a part seems better for this piece. Have them explain their answer.

5. Discuss with students the nature of polyphony and the advantage of a lighter, thinner texture of few voices.

Indicators of Success

- Students perform their parts effectively as part of a small ensemble with one student on a part.
- Students sing expressively, applying their knowledge about the social and historical setting of madrigals to their singing.

Follow-up

- Explore with students various combinations of small group versus full ensemble on the selected madrigal. Discuss with students which arrangement they find most effective. Then have students perform the madrigal accordingly in concert.

STANDARD 2B

Performing on instruments, alone and with others, a varied repertoire of music: Students perform an appropriate part in an ensemble, demonstrating well-developed ensemble skills.

Objective

- Students will perform in a percussion ensemble, making proper entrances, performing rhythms with precision, keeping a steady beat, and listening to other parts for appropriate balance.

Materials

- Assortment of drums, including conga
- *Agogos,* cowbells, or other bells—high and low sounds needed
- *Shekeres* (gourd rattles with a netted covering of beads) or other shakers

Prior Knowledge and Experiences

- Students have sung some African songs, such as the South African freedom song "Siyahamba."

Procedures

1. Review or teach students the basics of drumming: (a) tones—produced by hitting the drum with the fingers of a closed palm, pulling the high sounds out of the drum; (b) slaps—produced by hitting the drum with relaxed fingers so that it feels like a whipping motion (quite percussive compared to the tone) and ending with the fingers muting the drum; and (c) bass—produced by hitting the center of the drum with the full palm, pulling out the very low tones of the drum.

2. Introduce the following rhythmic ostinatos for the drums:

Select students to play the drums in a song accompaniment and divide drummers into two groups, assigning one of the ostinatos to each group. Then have drummers play the ostinatos together.

3. Add the following bell part:

4. Introduce the following part for the shakers, having students hold the instrument next to the thigh with one hand over the top so that the instrument can hit both the leg and the other hand.

5. As students create a percussion ensemble, encourage them to move their bodies so that they feel the rhythms throughout their entire bodies. Have the entire ensemble play together.

6. Have students sing a familiar African song, such as "Siyahamba," and accompany their singing with the percussion ensemble; adapt the rhythms for songs in other meters. Discuss with students the expressive markings in the selected song, emphasizing the importance of a uniform interpretation and of precise entrances and cut-offs in ensemble performance. Also, discuss the importance of listening to other parts and players. Then ask students to play and sing the piece again with more focus on listening to others.

7. Ask students to evaluate their own performance and that of the whole class and make suggestions for improvement. Have students keep the suggestions in mind and perform the piece once more, focusing on style and expression, as well as balance and blend.

Indicators of Success

- Students demonstrate improvement in their ensemble skills as they listen more to each other and focus on playing accurately and expressively.

Follow-up

- Using the same song or another song, ask individual students to improvise cadences, bridges, and solos in the percussion ensemble.

- Work with students to devise call-and-response warm-ups to be accompanied by the rhythms they have learned.

STANDARD 3A

Improvising melodies, variations, and accompaniments: Students improvise stylistically appropriate harmonizing parts.

Objective

- Students will improvise a stylistically appropriate four-part harmony to a South African protest song.

Materials

- "We Shall Not Give Up the Fight," from *Freedom Is Coming: Songs of Protest and Praise from South Africa* by Anders Nyberg, edited by Henry H. Leck (Fort Lauderdale, FL: Walton Music Corporation), WW1149, three-part, Level 2; WW1174, SAB, Level 2

- Copies of melody and words only for "We Shall Not Give Up the Fight"

- "Amazing Grace," arr. John Newton and Edward Lojeski (Milwaukee: Hal Leonard Corporation), 8300531, SATB, Level 1; or another four-part hymn arrangement

Prior Knowledge and Experiences

- Students have sung four-part harmony.

- Students have had some experience improvising four-part harmony.

Procedures

1. Distribute the arrangement of "Amazing Grace" and discuss with students the functions of voice parts as used in hymns. Ask students to identify which part carries the melody. Then have them define the harmonic role of the other three parts. Lead them to recognize that the alto line harmonizes (usually below) with the soprano, the tenor line fills out the harmony, and the bass line outlines the harmonic progression.

2. Give students the melody and words only for "We Shall Not Give Up the Fight," and teach them the melody. Explain briefly to students what this piece is about and the tradition from which it comes. Discuss with students what this tells them about the style in which the piece should be sung.

3. As sopranos sing the melody continuously, have basses improvise a bass line. Encourage each bass to find what sounds best to his ear. Although the piece may sound like a mess at first, basses will eventually relax and find a workable bass line. Remind them as they are working on it that it need not be fancy; it should simply set up a basic harmonic structure.

4. Once the bass line is clearer, have basses join sopranos, singing continuously, and ask altos to improvise their line. Remind altos that they should harmonize with the sopranos in thirds and fourths and sometimes even sing in unison; have them listen to each other in order to agree on a line. In the process, their line may occasionally split into two or more parts. Because it is likely that you will end up with a number of variations, ask some of your more confident singers to perform their improvisations for the class.

5. Finally, invite tenors to explore a line that fits in with the other three lines. By this point in the process, they should feel confident and their part should come easily.

6. Split the choir into quartets and ask individual quartets to sing for the class. After each performance, have students discuss the choices the quartet made and how it sounded to them, including whether the harmonization was stylistically appropriate, considering the tradition of the melody. Encourage each quartet to do something a little different (such as embellish the soprano line), and challenge the class to determine what that might be.

7. Give students the published arrangement of "We Shall Not Give Up the Fight," and have them sing it. Discuss with them the harmonization choices made by the arranger. Have them compare the style of their improvisations to that of the arranger.

Indicators of Success

- Students improvise a stylistically appropriate four-part harmony for a melody.

Follow-up

- Introduce songs and spirituals that require call-and-response techniques, and let students figure out how to respond to a call in two-, three-, or four-part harmony.

- Have students improvise descants or create their own arrangements of songs by varying the voices used.

- Have students listen to several arrangements of the same song to give them an appreciation of and ideas for improvising harmonies.

STANDARD 3B

Improvising melodies, variations, and accompaniments: Students improvise rhythmic and melodic variations on given pentatonic melodies and melodies in major and minor keys.

Objective

- Students will improvise melodic variations on a twelve-bar blues melody.

Materials

- Appropriate blues melody, with words, in the traditional three-phrase, twelve-bar blues structure.

Prior Knowledge and Experiences

- Students are familiar with the terms *riff* and *scat.*

Procedures

1. As a warm-up, have students sing and improvise on the melody of "Heart and Soul," using the syllable "bah," with enthusiastic style. This should be a fun and freeing warm-up, without many parameters. Model your own riffs and scat syllables to help students loosen up. Have various students provide piano accompaniment.

2. Teach students the melody to "Centerpiece" by ear. Then have them sing it as a group until they are comfortable with it and have it memorized.

3. After students have learned the piece, help them to discover the three-phrase, twelve-bar structure of the melody.

4. Invite students to experiment with the melody, "bending" it a little, stretching a word, changing a note, rushing a little, laying back a little, and so on. Tell them to try not to imitate the person next to them.

5. Have the choir count off by twos, and ask the number ones to sing the melody and the twos to add little scat "fills" between phrases or even during phrases. Tell students that they can use words from those singing the melody or, if they want to be daring, they can use all scat syllables. Limit their scat choices at first, however, to "bah" and "dah." Give both groups the opportunity to improvise.

6. Gradually, have those singing the melody substitute scat syllables for the text. Eventually, the original melody may disappear entirely, as well.

7. While students are singing, stop them occasionally and ask what they are doing to alter the melodic line or where they are getting ideas for their scat fills. After ideas have been shared, continue the process. Provide opportunities for soloists or solo groups to improvise this way also.

Indicators of Success

- Students improvise confidently and freely on a twelve-bar blues melody and provide scat fills between phrases.

Follow-up

- Introduce recordings of the same melody as sung by various artists, and discuss the differences in artists' embellishment and improvisational styles.

- Using other standard melodies, apply procedures similar to those outlined above. Introduce students to the concept of motives (rhythmic and melodic), and encourage them to borrow motives from the existing melody in their improvisations.

STANDARD 3C

Improvising melodies, variations, and accompaniments: *Students improvise original melodies over given chord progressions, each in a consistent style, meter, and tonality.*

Objective

- Students will create a riff over a blues progression.

Materials

- Recording of Jamey Aebersold's *Jazz: How to Play and Improvise,* vol. 1, Jamey Aebersold Jazz, PO Box 1244C, New Albany, IN 47151 (optional)
- Audio-playback equipment (if recording is used)

Prior Knowledge and Experiences

- Students have studied the blues progression.
- Students are familiar with scat syllables.
- Students have improvised scat "conversations," using the syllables "bah" and "dah," snapping on beats 2 and 4 in a given tempo, and carrying on a conversation at a loose rhythm. Through these conversations, they have learned to use their voices to make their improvisations interesting, becoming more flexible in their speaking (range, timbre, special vocal effects, etc.) and more rhythmic and creative.

Procedures

1. As a warm-up, engage students in a scat conversation (see Prior Knowledge and Experiences). Ask students different questions to which they must respond, and encourage them to make clear what they are talking about by inflection, gesture, facial expression, timbre, and so on.

2. Review the blues progression and discuss with students the blues style.

3. Introduce students to the term *riff,* demonstrating appropriately and explaining that it is a short, repeated melodic or rhythmic figure. Ask students to create a riff of their own, all at the same time, over the blues progression. Remind them that their riffs should be in the blues style and in the given meter and tonality. [*Note:* Play the progression on the piano, use a sequenced version, have a student (or a student combo) play it, or use the Aebersold recording.] Explain that their riffs need not be on one note, but one note is okay. After one repeat, have students try a new riff. Keep the music going, giving students three or four chances to create a riff.

4. While the large group keeps its riffs going, have two soloists "trade 2's," (that is, exchange, or trade, two-measure performed solos, actually conversing in scat). Help students, if necessary, to "feel" their two-bar solos, gesturing so that they know when to start and stop. Tell them that their conversations can overlap each other and that they can interrupt each other.

5. Have students limit their scat syllables to "bah" and "dah" if they are still insecure. To make them more comfortable, emphasize the conversational aspect of their improvisation with questions such as "What were you trying to say?" Continue the activity until all students get the chance to trade 2's.

Indicators of Success

- Students improvise riffs over a blues progression consistent with the blues style and in the appropriate meter and tonality.

Follow-up

- Expand this strategy to a four-bar or even a twelve-bar solo.

STANDARD 3D

Improvising melodies, variations, and accompaniments: Students improvise stylistically appropriate harmonizing parts in a variety of styles.

Objective

- Students will harmonize over a Baroque ground bass.

Materials

- Recording of Canon in D by Johann Pachelbel (the slower the better)
- Audio-playback equipment
- Notation for bass line of Canon in D (see music example)
- Chalkboard

Prior Knowledge and Experiences

- Students have studied the Baroque style and have sung music of the Baroque period.

Procedures

1. Write the bass line for Pachelbel's Canon in D on the chalkboard, as follows:

   During the warm-up, ask students to sightread the bass line.

2. Play the recording of the Canon in D, and ask students to identify which part is playing the melody (bass).

3. Ask students to sing the bass line on "loo" while listening to the recording to help them discover that this bass line repeats strictly. Introduce the term *ground bass*.

4. Ask students what makes the Canon in D interesting, and have them listen to several minutes of the recording with that question in mind. Then have them discuss their thoughts. Help students to consider what the other instruments are doing to make the piece interesting, asking them to be specific in their descriptions. Review with them the characteristics of Baroque music and help them relate the style of this piece to what they have learned. Lead them to discuss the tension between the strictness of the bass line and the imaginative freedom of the upper lines.

5. Explain to students that even though this piece is written out note-for-note, in Baroque performance practice, musicians often improvised on a bass line. So improvisation was a necessary skill for the Baroque musician.

6. Play the recording again and ask students to harmonize on "loo" with half notes that "sound good." Encourage them not to be afraid of wrong notes but to keep experimenting until they can hear which notes will work almost before they sing them. Remind them to listen for the ground bass and to try to not listen to those improvising around them. As students become more secure, invite them to add occasional quarter notes to "connect" their half notes.

7. At a certain point in the improvisation, cut out the recording and let students sing their improvisations unaccompanied.

(continued)

Indicators of Success

- Students confidently sing and improvise parts that harmonize with a Baroque ground bass and that fit the style of this Baroque music.

Follow-up

- Use a similar procedure to have students create an original four-measure ground bass. Then play the ground bass on the piano, have a student play it, or have a small group continue singing it as students improvise over it.

- Play a recorded example of a barbershop quartet selection and ask students to identify which vocal part has the melody [the lead]. If possible, provide scores for students to follow as they listen. Discuss with them how the harmonization of a barbershop quartet differs from that of the more traditional choral work. [The highest vocal part (tenor) does *not* maintain the melody.] Encourage students to listen for improvised vocal lines as well, since final cadences are often completely improvised.

STANDARD 3E

Improvising melodies, variations, and accompaniments: Students improvise original melodies in a variety of styles, over given chord progressions, each in a consistent style, meter, and tonality.

Objective

- Students will improvise melodies in the Baroque style.

Materials

- *Jazz Sebastian Bach,* performed by the Swingle Singers, Philips 824-703-2

- Bach selection that uses a ground bass—for example, "Meine Tage in dem Leide," from Cantata 150 by Johann Sebastian Bach (Miami: Warner Bros. Publications), K06056, SATB, Level 3–4; or "Cruci-fixus," from Mass in B minor, by J. S. Bach (Milwaukee: Hal Leonard Corporation), 08678813, SATB, Level 4

- Chalkboard

- Audio-playback equipment

Prior Knowledge and Experiences

- Students have been rehearsing the Bach choral selection.

- Students have studied ground bass and are familiar with the term.

Procedures

1. Play any selection from *Jazz Sebastian Bach* that has an obvious motivic structure—for example, "Prelude en Fa Majeur," "Fugue en Do Mineur," or "Invention en Do Majeur." Ask students to describe Bach's melody.

2. Help students discover characteristics of Baroque melody from what they have learned about Bach's melody; that is, the melody is built from short motives, it is long and spinning out, and it is very ornamented. List the characteristics on the chalkboard and discuss them with students, as necessary, until they have a clear understanding of the characteristics of Baroque melodies.

3. Review the ground bass in the Bach choral work that the choir has been rehearsing. Ask students to sing the ground bass until they have memorized it. Play it on the piano while students improvise their own Baroque melody above it, using scat syllables such as "doo" and "doobee" or "bah" and "bah-dah." Encourage them to keep in mind the characteristics on the board and to try different motives until they find one that they can develop and embellish.

4. Have volunteers sing their improvisations for the class while the rest of the class sings the ground bass.

Indicators of Success

- Students improvise melodies in a typical Baroque style over a ground bass.

- Students describe some general characteristics of Baroque melodic style using appropriate terminology.

Follow-up

- When students perform in a concert the Bach selection used in the procedures outlined above, have them improvise, as above, and explain the process to the audience in a kind of "informance."

- In subsequent rehearsals, play examples with a ground bass from *Jazz Sebastian Bach* and have students improvise melodies on the ground.

(continued)

- Introduce the idea of ornamentation and help students to hear ornaments in various recordings of Baroque music. Encourage students to experiment vocally with the ideas they hear.

- Play a recording for students of the fourth movement of Brahms's Symphony no. 4, and have them compare how a Romantic composer writing for orchestra built variations on the same ground bass as Bach used in "Meine Tage in dem Leide."

Proficient

STANDARD 4A

Composing and arranging music within specified guidelines: _Students compose music in several distinct styles, demonstrating creativity in using the elements of music for expressive effect._

Objective

- Students will begin to compose by completing musical periods.

Materials

- Chalkboard
- Manuscript paper
- Sightsinging text (optional for example; see step 1)

Prior Knowledge and Experiences

- Students can sightread music with a level of difficulty of 1 or 2.
- Students have basic notation skills.

Procedures

1. Write on the chalkboard a musical antecedent ("question") phrase with an unfinished consequent ("answer") phrase. For example:

2. Briefly review with students the key, tonal center, and meter of the example and then ask them to sightread it.
3. Ask each student to compose a logical ending to the phrase, notating the ending on manuscript paper.
4. Ask individual students either to write their endings on the board for all to sing or to sing their endings alone or with a friend after the choir sings the first half. After each demonstration, discuss with students their reactions to what they hear. Ask them whether the ending was logical, what made it logical, how it tied in with the antecedent phrase, and in what way it was interesting.
5. Through discussion, help students to focus on the aspects of repetition (unity) and contrast (variety) as necessary elements, even in composing a short melody like this.

Indicators of Success

- Students create logical and interesting endings to consequent phrases in response to given antecedent phrases.

Follow-up

- Challenge students weekly with increasingly more difficult and unpredictable phrases in various keys and meters. Through discussion, help them discover basic principles of effective melodic composition. Then have students improvise their melodies by turning this strategy into a call-and-response activity.

Composing and arranging music within specified guidelines: Students compose music in several distinct styles, demonstrating creativity in using the elements of music for expressive effect.

Objective

- Students will create and perform aleatoric, or chance, music using nonstandard notation, showing understanding of both the aleatoric concept and the musical elements with which they are working.

Materials

- Large sheets of paper
- Crayons, markers, or colored pencils
- Chalkboard
- "Miniwanka" by R. Murray Schafer (Indian River, Ontario, Canada: Arcana Editions), treble voices alone or SATB, Level 2

Prior Knowledge and Experiences

- Students have studied the elements of music and have explored various compositional structures.
- Students are familiar with the terms *phrase, cadence, contour, tempo,* and *dynamics.*

Procedures

1. Ask students to describe the many "moments," or states, of water. Encourage them to be creative and innovative in their thinking. As students share terms such as "steam," "ice," "showers," "fizz," "sweat," write them on the chalkboard.

2. Have students describe how the moment of "fizz" might sound. Encourage them to explore the full sound range of the term. For example, ask them whether fizz always sounds the same or whether there are moments of less or greater fizz.

3. Divide the choir into small groups and provide them with paper and colored writing utensils. Ask each group to choose a moment of water from the board, determine how it might sound, as they did with fizz, and then "notate" it by illustrating it. Encourage students to explore all sound makers available to them (e.g., bodies, floors, pencils, shoes) and include them in their "notation," in addition to exploring the full range of the "moment" (some choreography might even be appropriate). Review the elements of music and ask students to consider what they know about how the elements can be used to unify and vary their compositions. Encourage students to use appropriate music vocabulary for the terms phrase, cadence, contour, tempo, and dynamics.

4. When the groups are finished, have each group perform its moment for the class. Tell the performing group to first tape its illustration on the board for everyone to see and not to tell the class what moment they chose so that students will have to listen carefully. Allow the class a few moments to read the notation before the group performs. After each performance, have the class guess the moment being performed and give reasons (both visual and auditory) for their guesses.

5. Introduce the term *aleatoric* and the concept of no two performances sounding alike. You might also discuss with students whether any two performances ever sound alike and under what circumstances this is desirable or undesirable.

6. Distribute copies of "Miniwanka" and ask students to glance through the score and determine (without spending too much time looking at the words) what this piece is about. Chronicle with them the moments of water Schafer chose to notate and the musical gestures he used to do so, comparing these with their own compositions. If students develop several interpretations, ask them to determine which one to pursue in their performance of the work.

Indicators of Success

- Students use the elements of music creatively to compose aleatoric music.

- Students demonstrate their understanding of aleatoric music in their compositions and in interpreting nonstandard notation.

Follow-up

- Ask one student (or perhaps a small group of students) to be a composer and put the individual notations from this lesson in a specific order to create a composition. Inform students that there should be reasons for the chosen order and that they will be asked to explain their reasons to the class. Ask the class to perform the composition by having each group perform their moment at the appropriate time. When finished, ask the class if the composition "worked," telling them to consider what they know about the elements of music.

- Have students create other short compositions using the procedure in step 3, but this time have the small groups exchange notations before they are performed, keeping their particular subjects a secret. Once the groups have studied each other's illustrations, ask individual groups to perform for the class. After students have attempted to guess the subject, ask the performers to explain their interpretive choices. Then allow the composers to perform their illustrations. Discuss what caused differences in the performances, making sure students refer to the notation.

Composing and arranging music within specified guidelines: Students arrange pieces for voices or instruments other than those for which the pieces were written in ways that preserve or enhance the expressive effect of the music.

Objective

- Students will arrange a piano composition for voices or for solo voice and piano.

Materials

- Recording of "Adagio for Strings" by Samuel Barber
- "Agnus Dei" by Samuel Barber (Milwaukee: Hal Leonard Corporation), HL50313910, SATB, Level 6
- Recordings and sheet music for three or four short piano pieces with lyrical melodies—for example, Felix Mendelssohn's *Songs without Words* or selections from Robert Schumann's *Scenes from Childhood* or *Album for the Young*
- Audio-playback equipment
- Manuscript paper

Prior Knowledge and Experiences

- Students can read notation with a difficulty level of 2 or 3.
- Students have studied music notation.
- Students know the ranges of vocal parts and have written simple vocal arrangements.

Procedures

1. Play "Adagio for Strings" for students, sharing pertinent background information. For example, explain that it is Barber's orchestral transcription of the second movement of a string quartet he wrote in 1936. Discuss with students aspects of the work's construction, such as the number of parts (four to six), its organization (one melody passed from part to part in a musical sequence), and its overall mood (intense, emotional).

2. Have students look at the score of Barber's choral arrangement "Agnus Dei" and compare it with his "Adagio for Strings." Discuss with students why Barber chose this text for his choral arrangement and what changes he made in adapting the original string version for voices.

3. Play for students recordings of three or four short Mendelssohn or Schumann piano pieces with lyrical melodies and descriptive titles. Provide students with the music for these works (or other works in the public domain) and have students choose one that interests them and begin writing an arrangement of it with an original text, inspired by the title or mood. Depending on students' ability levels, the arrangements could vary from solo voice and piano to a full unaccompanied arrangement of three to five voice parts.

4. Have students evaluate their own work or other students' work for effectiveness. Remind them that they should consider how the arrangements preserve or enhance the expressive effect of the original work.

Indicators of Success

- Students create effective vocal, or vocal and piano, arrangements of short piano pieces.
- Students describe how their arrangements preserve or enhance the expressive effect of the original works.

Follow-up

- Play for students other vocal arrangements of instrumental works—e.g., the Swingle Singers' arrangements of the music of Bach, Mozart (such as *The Swingle Singers: A Cappella Amadeus,* Virgin Classics Limited CD 0777 7596172 0), Handel, and Vivaldi. Also, play the original instrumental versions. Discuss with students the techniques used by the arranger in adapting these works for voices.

- Have students perform their arrangements in class or in concert.

STANDARD 4B

Composing and arranging music within specified guidelines: Students arrange pieces for voices or instruments other than those for which the pieces were written in ways that preserve or enhance the expressive effect of the music.

Objective

■ Students will arrange a choral work for instruments.

Materials

■ English madrigal in the public domain

■ Recordings that combine voices and instruments in Renaissance vocal music

■ Audio-playback equipment

■ Chalkboard

■ Manuscript paper

Prior Knowledge and Experiences

■ Students have been rehearsing the selected madrigal.

■ Students can read notation with a difficulty level of 2 or 3.

■ Students have studied music notation.

■ Students have had experience transposing melodies on manuscript paper in both treble and bass clefs.

Procedures

1. Have students listen as you play a recording of a Renaissance work that combines voices and instruments. Explain the Renaissance practice of seeing voices and instruments as equal and the common substitution of instruments for missing voices.

2. Through recordings, familiarize students with typical Renaissance instruments, their timbres, and their modern equivalents, and help them discover the characteristic uses of instruments in Renaissance practice—for example, brass and/or string "choirs" that alternated with or doubled the vocal parts in church music; consorts that accompanied or substituted for voices in secular madrigals. Ask students who play any of these instruments to raise their hands, and write their names, their instruments, and the performing ranges and key transpositions of their instruments on the board.

3. Ask students to begin arranging the English madrigal they have been rehearsing for instruments for which players are available, keeping in mind what they have just discussed about the instruments. Explain that they will have to make choices about which instruments to assign to which voice parts and what combinations of instruments (string, brass, or wind) will be most authentic or effective. Note that they could plan to have the instruments perform *colla voce* (with the voices) or in alternating verses.

Indicators of Success

■ Students create effective instrumental arrangements, demonstrating their understanding of Renaissance performance practice, and of correct range, transposition, and idiosyncrasies of the instruments they choose.

Follow-up

■ In subsequent classes, have students perform the arrangements. Have them discuss the effectiveness of each arrangement, including the choice of instruments used in the arrangements.

STANDARD 4B

Composing and arranging music within specified guidelines: Students arrange pieces for voices or instruments other than those for which the pieces were written in ways that preserve or enhance the expressive effect of the music.

Objective

- Students create medley arrangements around a theme.

Materials

- Choral arrangement that combines several folk songs or that is a medley of pop, show, or folk melodies
- Books of folk songs, show tunes, and pop songs
- Chalkboard

Prior Knowledge and Experiences

- Students have been rehearsing the selected choral arrangement.

Procedures

1. Using the medley or arrangement that students have been rehearsing, help them discover characteristics of medley arrangements—the ebb and flow in moods, transitional material that links contrasting melodies, key relationships, contrasts in texture, unifying devices. List these general principles on the chalkboard as students identify them.

2. Have students peruse the collections of folk songs, show tunes, and pop songs to look for common themes that interest them (such as unrequited love, the railroad, wanting to fly, rivers, songs about dancing, musical show tunes about teenagers).

3. Ask each student, or group of students, to sketch out a medley of three to six songs for the selected theme. Depending on their ability, the sketch could vary from a simple prose outline describing the sound of the arrangement to a full arrangement in notation.

4. Discuss with students the unique features of medleys.

Indicators of Success

- Students identify and describe characteristics of medleys and how they can preserve or enhance the expressive effect of the music.
- Students plan arrangements that are constructed logically and expressively and that make good use of the selected songs.

Follow-up

- In subsequent classes, have students work on their arrangements. When they have completed them, give students the opportunity to compare their arrangements, discussing the effectiveness of student choices in arranging.

Composing and arranging music within specified guidelines: *Students arrange pieces for voices or instruments other than those for which the pieces were written in ways that preserve or enhance the expressive effect of the music.*

Objective

- Students will create four-part choral arrangements of a folk song.

Materials

- Several choral arrangements of "Shenandoah"—e.g., arr. James Erb (New York: Lawson-Gould Music Publishers/Alfred Publishing Company), 04-51846, SSAATTBB, Level 3; or arr. Mary Goetze (New York: Boosey & Hawkes), OCTB6257, SSA, Level 3
- Several books of folk songs
- Manuscript paper

Prior Knowledge and Experiences

- Students have discussed features of an arrangement of a folk song they have sung.
- Students have studied music notation.

Procedures

1. Introduce students to the melody only of "Shenandoah" by playing it on the piano and having them sing it back to you.

2. When students are familiar with the melody, distribute the choral arrangements of the song. Discuss the arrangements with students, having them compare the arrangers' choices and look for similarities and differences. Lead students to discover the effect of many parts versus the effect of a single voice part. Ask students why they think the arrangers made the choices they made.

3. Assign students a specific folk song to arrange for voices, or have students peruse the folk song collections and ask each student to choose one folk song to arrange.

4. Have students create their own four-part choral arrangement of the selected folk song. Depending on students' individual ability, they could sketch the arrangement or create and notate a complete arrangement. Tell students to be ready to articulate the logic of their choices when they submit their arrangements or plans.

Indicators of Success

- Students create or plan folk song arrangements that are logically crafted and expressive.

Follow-up

- Have students compare their arrangements, performing them in class, if possible, and discuss the effectiveness of students' choices in arranging.

STANDARD 4C

Composing and arranging music within specified guidelines: *Students compose and arrange music for voices and various acoustic and electronic instruments, demonstrating knowledge of the ranges and traditional usages of the sound sources.*

Objective

■ Students compose an instrumental descant for a folk melody.

Materials

■ "Ca' the Yowes," arr. Mary Goetze (New York: Boosey & Hawkes), 6258, SA, Level 3; or another folk song with an instrumental descant, such as "The Turtle Dove," arr. Linda Steen Spevacek (Milwaukee: Jenson/Hal Leonard Corporation), 43725024, SATB with flute, Level 3

■ Another folk song in any form

■ Worksheet with list of questions (see step 1)

■ Manuscript paper

Prior Knowledge and Experiences

■ Students have studied music notation.

■ Students have learned the selected folk song with an instrumental descant.

Procedures

1. Have students sing "Ca' the Yowes" with one student performing the instrumental descant. Then distribute the worksheet with the following questions:

   ■ What instrument did the arranger choose and why?

   ■ How is the melodic/motivic material of the descant related to the folk song melody?

   ■ How does the descant interlock with the vocal parts? For example, Where in the phrases is the descant most active? How and where does the descant appear? How does the descant highlight the folk melody? How does it provide contrast with the melody? How does it provide unity with the melody?

2. Ask students to look at their music and, using the questions on the worksheet, analyze in a group discussion the instrumental descant in "Ca' the Yowes." Suggest to students that they take notes on the discussion. [*Note:* Make sure students have had plenty of opportunities to hear the descant before attempting this class discussion.]

3. Introduce another folk song, distributing copies of it to students.

4. Ask students to compose an appropriate instrumental descant for the new folk song. Tell them to consider all of the questions and their notes from their discussion on "Ca' the Yowes" in making their arranging choices. Remind them to be ready to explain their choices.

5. Have a volunteer play (or you play) his or her descant for the class and, if time allows, have the class discuss its strong points, considering the earlier discussion about instrumental descants.

Indicators of Success

■ Students create instrumental descants that are expressive, technically correct, and musically satisfying.

Follow-up

■ Have students perform the various descants they have composed, and after each performance, ask the class to discuss the effectiveness of the students' compositional choices.

(continued)

■ If the folk song that was used is strophic, ask students to make a sketch or plan of a full choral arrangement, deciding how each verse should be arranged. Some students may create full choral arrangements.

STANDARD 4D

Composing and arranging music within specified guidelines: Students compose music, demonstrating imagination and technical skill in applying the principles of composition.

Objective

- Students will compose a choral work based on a madrigal using extended vocal techniques.

Materials

- "April Is in My Mistress' Face" by Thomas Morley (Boston: E. C. Schirmer), 1612, SATB, Level 3; or another Renaissance madrigal with descriptive or narrative text, text painting, or rich imagery

- Manuscript paper

Prior Knowledge and Experiences

- Students have memorized "April Is in my Mistress' Face."

- Students have analyzed an exemplary string quartet of the Classical period, answering questions about the instrumentation, the time in which the music was written, the form, and compositional techniques characteristic of the four parts.

Procedures

1. Divide students into quartets or double quartets.

2. Have each small group "deconstruct" the madrigal by pulling apart its various musical elements, moods, and musical gestures, and then "reconstruct" it as a new piece in a twentieth-century style. For example, they may manipulate tempos, dynamics, articulation, melodic details, harmonies, rhythms, vocal colors, and textures in any way to enhance or alter the piece's meaning or effect. They may alter the form or use repetition, additions, or deletions. They may use extended vocal techniques (such as clicking, popping, humming, or speaking) and any other supplementary sounds they can perform (including body percussion), as well as movement. Their task is to create a new piece, using the old piece as raw material, either enhancing the old piece's meaning or changing it.

3. Remind students of the vast differences they discovered between the Classical quartet and the twentieth-century string quartet they heard. Encourage them to push the limits of their imagination, using the madrigal in any way they like and using its text as a framework and inspiration for their ideas.

4. Have students record their ideas using standard or nonstandard notation, or both.

Indicators of Success

- Students work cooperatively to create effective and imaginative compositions.

- Students perform their compositions and discuss the effectiveness of their compositional choices.

Follow-up

- Show students examples of twentieth-century works using non-standard notation or other extended vocal techniques. Discuss the effectiveness of various techniques, encouraging the discussion with questions such as "What is music?" and "What makes good music?"

(continued)

- Students have compared the traditional characteristics of the Classical string quartet with the nontraditional sounds of the twentieth-century string quartet by George Crumb on *Black Angels,* performed by the Kronos Quartet, Elektra Nonesuch 9 79242-2.

Proficient

STANDARD 5A

Reading and notating music: Students demonstrate the ability to read an instrumental or vocal score of up to four staves by describing how the elements of music are used.

Objective

■ Students will mark and read all four staves of their vocal scores, describing how the elements of music are used.

Materials

■ Choral piece in four parts

Prior Knowledge and Experiences

■ Students have studied basic rhythm and tonal patterns.

■ Students have experience using solfège.

■ Students can read the treble and bass clef and can follow their own parts with little difficulty.

■ Students have rehearsed the first page of the selected four-part choral piece, but they have not read the rest of the work.

Procedures

1. Have students begin to sing through the selected choral piece. When a section breaks down, stop and help that section discover another part that sang the same pitch earlier so they can find their pitches.

2. As they and other sections need help, encourage them to scan all parts, transposing clefs as necessary to identify pitches in common among several parts. Tell students to circle the notes giving them difficulty as well as the notes in other parts that can help them. Then have them draw connecting lines to show the related notes.

3. In parts of the music that are imitative, have students identify any motives as they pass among the parts, drawing a "connect the dots" line between the parts to show how the imitation is passed among the parts. Ask students questions that help them see how the elements of music, such as melody, are used, as well as questions that guide them to think about how the elements relate to one another; for example, "How does the timbre change when the melody moves to the tenor voice?"

4. Remind students that they should always know what is happening in other parts during the rehearsal. When the choir stops singing in rehearsal, quiz students about what is happening among the parts and encourage them to be aware of the pitch relationships among the parts; for example: "Altos, who else has C# here?" Even in a homophonic chord, make students aware of what other part might share a pitch and emphasize the importance of being aware of this visually and aurally for intonation.

5. Occasionally ask students to open to a page of their scores and hold it up so you can observe if they are indeed marking their scores.

Indicators of Success

■ Students begin to read all staves of a choral piece and mark their parts accordingly as they discover relationships between the parts.

■ Students demonstrate their understanding of how the elements of music are used in a choral piece.

(continued)

Follow-up

- Encourage students to invent and share with the class other score-marking strategies.

- Give students a new piece with four staves and have them mark their music and then attempt to sightread it.

STANDARD 5B

Reading and notating music: Students sightread, accurately and expressively, music with a level of difficulty of 3, on a scale of 1 to 6.

Objective

- Students will sightread a choral score with a level of difficulty of 3.

Materials

- Choral selection, unfamiliar to students, with a clear tonal center and a difficulty level of 3

Prior Knowledge and Experiences

- Students can sing and identify basic rhythm and tonal patterns.
- Students have experience using solfège.

Procedures

1. Have each student look at his or her copy of the selected piece. As you sing one of the lines in the piece on solfège or a neutral syllable, ask students to listen and identify which line you are singing.

2. If students do not guess the line you are singing right away, guide them to spot tell-tale rhythms or tonal patterns in the notation.

3. To teach them to follow the notes, sing the line again and stop somewhere in the middle, asking students to indicate where you stopped.

4. If the music presents particularly challenging rhythms for students, have them read the lines with such rhythms silently, snapping on just the quarter notes in each measure. To train their eyes and ears, have them do the same thing again, tapping or speaking "ti-ti" on the eighth notes only (everything else is silent). When their rhythm is secure, move on.

5. Have students identify the tonal center of the piece and draw boxes around all the *do*s. Then have them sing only the *do*s while you sing everything else.

6. Have students circle all the *sol*s and then sing all *do*s and *sol*s while you sing the rest. Now that they have heard the phrase several times in several ways, have them try to sing the entire phrase. If they cannot yet sing the entire phrase correctly, add one more prominent pitch to the notes they sing while you continue to sing everything else.

7. Use the same process to guide students in reading the next phrase.

Indicators of Success

- Students identify the tonal center of a choral score and use it to guide them in their sightreading.
- Students sightread a choral score with increased confidence.

Follow-up

- Each day, give students a line or more to sightread from either sightreading exercises or new choral repertoire, encouraging them to use the skills they learned in this lesson.

STANDARD 5B

Reading and notating music: Students sightread, accurately and expressively, music with a level of difficulty of 3, on a scale of 1 to 6.

Objective

- Students will sightread a melody with a level of difficulty of 3 and transpose it from treble to bass clef.

Materials

- Music for a melody with a level of difficulty of 3 from a choral piece that is unfamiliar to students or a sightreading exercise
- Chalkboard (optional)
- Manuscript paper

Prior Knowledge and Experiences

- Students can identify the names of the lines and spaces in both treble and bass clef.
- Students have had some experience sightreading in both clefs.
- Students have basic notation skills.

Procedures

1. Distribute to students a sheet with the selected melody in treble clef, or write it on the chalkboard.

2. Have students sightread the melody and then transpose it down one octave into bass clef on their manuscript paper. Walk around the classroom and check students' transpositions.

3. Use a similar process with a melody in the bass clef, having students transpose it to the treble clef.

4. When students are able to sightread and then transpose melodies from treble to bass and bass to treble clefs successfully, have them listen to a melody you sing and write it in either or both clefs. Do the same with other melodies.

5. After several melodies have been written, have students sing them as further sightreading practice.

6. Discuss with students how their ability to transpose will help them in their sightreading. Lead them to understand that they will need to find passages similar to those in their own choral parts in other voice parts, sometimes in a different clef than the one used for their own parts.

Indicators of Success

- Students sightread melodies and transpose them from both treble and bass clefs quickly and accurately.

Follow-up

- Distribute eight- to sixteen-measure sample sightreading exercises to students. Give them a minute to study the passage of their choice and then encourage them to sing the exercises individually. Begin with simple melismatic exercises and progress accordingly.

Reading and notating music: Students sightread, accurately and expressively, music with a level of difficulty of 3, on a scale of 1 to 6.

Objective

- Students will sightread four-measure vocal warm-ups, with a level of difficulty of 3, that their classmates have created and notated.

Materials

- Manuscript paper
- Chalkboard

Prior Knowledge and Experiences

- Students can sightread notation with a difficulty level of 2.
- Students have basic notation skills.
- Students have composed simple melodies.

Procedures

1. Ask each student to compose a moderately easy four-measure vocal warm-up vocalise. Set parameters as to range, style, and so on.

2. Choose one or two students to notate their warm-ups on the chalkboard.

3. Have the choir examine the warm-ups on the board silently for notational accuracy (that is, number of beats, correct use of rests, direction of stems, and so on).

4. Ask student composers to teach their warm-ups, helping the choir to sightsing them accurately and expressively, but not singing them or playing them on the piano for the choir. Suggest that they might remind the choir to check for repeated notes and ascending or descending intervals (both by step and skip), as well as rhythmic similarities with other parts or repeated rhythms within the same part.

5. After students have sightread the vocalises and warmed up with them, have the class evaluate the accuracy of the notation in conveying the composer's intentions. Give composers the opportunity to make adjustments to the vocalises, if necessary.

Indicators of Success

- Students create and write moderately easy four-bar vocalises for the class to sightread.
- Students sightread four-measure vocalises accurately and expressively.

Follow-up

- Have students practice writing notation from aural dictation, with you playing the piano, or have them write entire melodies for class sightsinging practice.

STANDARD 5D

Reading and notating music: Students interpret nonstandard notation symbols used by some 20th-century composers.

Objective

- Students will interpret non-standard notation used in a 20th-century choral composition, comparing it to symbols they have created to represent a choral exercise.

Materials

- "Epitaph for Moonlight" by R. Murray Schafer (Toronto: Berandol Music), BER1094, SSSSAAAATTTTBBBB, Level 5
- Student journals or portfolios

Prior Knowledge and Experiences

- Students are proficient at reading standard notation.
- Students can define and sing chromatic scales.

Procedures

1. Ask students to sing a descending chromatic scale on "loo" or "doo."

2. Divide each of the four sections (SATB) into four groups and number the groups (Soprano I, II, III, and IV, etc.) to create sixteen parts. Have the entire choir sing a descending chromatic scale of a tenth, each group singing one note, beginning with Soprano I and ending with Bass IV. Repeat the exercise until they can do it successfully.

3. Have students sing the exercise again, this time sustaining their notes to create a sixteen-part tone cluster. When they have done that successfully, have them repeat the exercise, this time humming their notes.

4. Have students hum the descending chromatic scale once more. This time, tell them to crescendo their tone-cluster hum until your cutoff, at which point everyone should stop singing except Alto I, Alto IV, and Tenor IV, which will leave a major triad. Repeat this exercise as needed. When students can sing it successfully, have them visualize the sound they are making.

5. Have students draw a representation of their visualization in their journals or portfolios. When they have finished drawing, have one or two volunteers share their graphics with the rest of the class, explaining why they drew what they did.

6. Distribute "Epitaph for Moonlight" and ask students to find a section that looks similar to their graphics (first two pages). Have them compare the representation with their graphics and then sing the first two pages of the piece, interpreting the nonstandard notation.

7. Have students peruse the rest of the score of "Epitaph for Moonlight" to become familiar with the graphic notation. Through discussion, help them discover the limitations of traditional notation in representing some 20th-century music and the need for imagination in notating it and in interpreting the notation for performance.

Indicators of Success

- Students create their own nonstandard notation symbols for the choral exercise they have sung.

- Students demonstrate their understanding of the graphics for a tone cluster used in the opening section of the selected piece, successfully singing that section.

Follow-up

- To introduce students to similar works by R. Murray Schafer, as they continue learning "Epitaph for Moonlight," use the recording *A Garden of Bells: Choral Music of R. Murray Schafer*, Vancouver Chamber Choir, Jon Washburn, Grouse Records 101 (Arcana Editions, Box 425, Station K, Toronto, Ont., Canada M4P 2G9).

STANDARD 5E

Reading and notating music: Students sightread, accurately and expressively, music with a level of difficulty of 4, on a scale of 1 to 6.

Objective

- Students will sightread accurately and expressively music with a level of difficulty of 4, working in pairs and coaching each other.

Materials

- Handouts with compilation of prepared sightsinging exercises (i.e., ten to twelve sixteen-measure exercises with phrasing indicated) with a level of difficulty of 4

- Two or three different handouts with several of the above exercises (see step 2)

- Set of cards with musical symbols and another set with the matching symbol name

Prior Knowledge and Experiences

- Students have sung scales and intervals using solfège syllables.

- Students can successfully sightread examples with a level of difficulty of 3.

Procedures

1. Pair students by randomly handing out the musical symbol cards and asking each student to find the person with the matching card.

2. Give each pair of students a different handout with a prepared sightsinging exercise and tell them to practice cooperatively. Tell students that their objective is to be able to sing the assigned exercises accurately and with expression.

3. Once the pairs are feeling confident, tell them to pretest each other, offering exaggerated praise and encouragement. [*Note:* This cooperative learning technique, called "pairs check," helps the groups monitor their work; the praise is a confidence builder and helps establish a supportive atmosphere.] Continually circulate, listen, and monitor students' progress.

4. Distribute a compilation of the prepared samples to the entire choir and ask students to sightread them with attention to expression.

Indicators of Success

- Students accurately sing any music example they have been sightreading when selected randomly by teacher circulating among teams.

Follow-up

- Use a similar strategy throughout the year with more and more difficult exercises. Have students, working in pairs, assess their particular sightsinging difficulties and prescribe the kinds of exercises they need in order to progress.

STANDARD 6A

Listening to, analyzing, and describing music: Students analyze aural examples of a varied repertoire of music, representing diverse genres and cultures, by describing the uses of elements of music and expressive devices.

Objective

- Students will analyze recorded examples of different vocal tone colors representing several different cultures.

Materials

- Recordings by choral groups and soloists with various vocal timbres, such as an English boys' choir; adult women with warm, dark sound—for example, *A Cathedral Concert,* performed by the Bulgarian State Radio and Television Female Choir, Verve World 314-510794-2; an opera chorus; or Tibetan monks
- Audio-playback equipment
- Paper
- Chalkboard with list of adjectives from which students may choose (see step 2)

Prior Knowledge and Experiences

- Students can use appropriate terminology to describe specific music events in a given aural example.

Procedures

1. Play recorded excerpts for students and ask them to write down for each excerpt whom they think is singing (men or women, young or old, and so on) and from what part of the world they think the music originates. Play the excerpts from the more familiar Western vocal styles and then move on to other world cultures.

2. Have students also write down adjectives to describe the tone color they hear for each piece (e.g., boys' choir: "pure, light, thin").

3. After all the examples have been played, discuss with students their responses to the music. Help them to focus on aspects of tone production that make each sound unique (nasality, use of vibrato, and so on), and help them place the different vocal styles/tone colors in a historical or cultural milieu by telling them who sang each.

4. Play different pieces by the same ensembles or with similar tone colors and have students try to identify them based on discussion of the previous examples.

Indicators of Success

- Students identify the difference in tone colors between English boys' choirs, opera choruses, and non-Western singers, and use words such as "vibrato" to describe them accurately.

Follow-up

- Lead a discussion about the various recordings used in this lesson with regard to students' individual preferences for vocal tone color. Invite students to share definitions of "beautiful" tone. Ask them how the concept of "beautiful" changes in different contexts and cultures.

STANDARD 6B

Listening to, analyzing, and describing music: Students demonstrate extensive knowledge of the technical vocabulary of music.

Objective

■ Students will demonstrate understanding of the terms *homophonic, polyphonic,* and *monophonic* by identifying these musical textures aurally and in notation.

Materials

■ "Hallelujah Chorus," from *Messiah,* by George Frideric Handel (New York: Carl Fischer), CM86, SATB, Level 5; or any Baroque chorus that mixes homophony and polyphony

■ Chalkboard

■ Call chart (on board or worksheets)

Prior Knowledge and Experiences

■ Students are familiar with the term *texture.*

■ Students can read notation proficiently.

Procedures

1. Have students sing through the first forty measures of "Hallelujah Chorus."

2. Draw the following two icons on the chalkboard:

A) B)

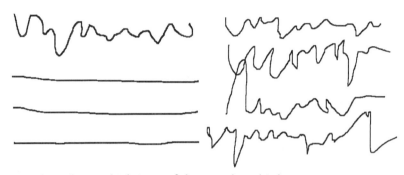

Ask students which icon of the two they think represents measures 4–11 and which represents 22–32. Allow students to discuss their thoughts. Help them focus on the importance of the soprano line compared to the others in measures 4–11 (icon A) versus the equality of melodic material in measures 22–32 (icon B). Introduce the terms homophonic (measures 4–11) and polyphonic (measures 22–32), and guide students in creating their own definitions.

3. Draw the following icon on the chalkboard:

Ask students which section of the piece this icon best represents. Remind them that it represents only the texture, not the shape of the melody. When they conclude that this icon represents measures 12–14—"for the Lord God"—ask them what term would fit this unison vocal line (monophonic). Help students to create a definition of monophonic.

4. Work with students to fill in a call chart, which divides the piece by sections. [*Note:* This can be done at the chalkboard or with students working individually on worksheets.] The call chart should list the sections or measure numbers and leave blanks for students to fill in the terms homophonic, polyphonic, or monophonic.

Indicators of Success

- Students define and identify homophonic, polyphonic, and monophonic textures aurally and in notation.

Follow-up

- Continue to explore aspects of these textures in other repertoire being rehearsed and in occasional listening examples. Help students to see various approaches to texture as a music history style marker. Ask, "What is an advantage of homophonic music for the listener?" (it's easier to understand the words); "What is an advantage of polyphonic music?" (exciting textures, all parts have interesting melodic material).

Proficient

STANDARD 6C

Listening to, analyzing, and describing music: *Students identify and explain compositional devices and techniques used to provide unity and variety and tension and release in a musical work and give examples of other works that make similar uses of these devices and techniques.*

Objective

- Students will identify pedal point as a tension device and explain its function in a musical selection.

Materials

- "Take, O Take Those Lips Away," from *Three Madrigals,* by Emma Lou Diemer (New York: Boosey & Hawkes), OCTB5417, SATB, Level 3; or another work that uses pedal point
- Chalkboard

Prior Knowledge and Experiences

- Students have been rehearsing the selected piece.

Procedures

1. Initiate a lighthearted discussion of tension. Ask students how they create tension at home (come home at 1:00 a.m. on a school night, and so on).

2. Continue the discussion by asking students how they think composers create tension in music. As students share their answers (extreme dynamics, marked articulations, dissonance, etc.), have one student write them on the chalkboard. If no student says "repeated notes," begin playing repeated quarter notes on a low C on the piano while you are guiding the discussion. When students make it clear that they are feeling the tension and irritation of your repeated notes, explain the concept of pedal point. Ask students to speculate on where the term comes from. Then explain that it originated with organ improvisations over a held pedal note.

3. To illustrate pedal point being used as a kind of dissonance, create a four-part chord and ask basses to sustain their note while the other three parts move up and down by half and whole steps at your direction. Explain that a pedal need not be in the lowest voice (although it often is), and try each of the other parts as the pedal, while the other voices move to dissonant chords.

4. Tell students to look at their copies of "Take, O Take" to discover where the pedal points are and which part has them. Have them offer suggestions as to what kind of tension is being created at the various pedal points and why the composer might have wanted tension.

5. To illustrate for students the unique musical "release" when a pedal tone finally changes, have them sing through the piece and listen for the tension and the release.

Indicators of Success

- Students sing and identify aurally and visually pedal point in music they are rehearsing.
- Students explain the function of pedal point as a tension device.

Follow-up

■ Give students opportunities to hear and sing pedal point in other situations and voice parts by incorporating examples into warm-up exercises as well as searching for them within the music already being rehearsed from various style periods (e.g., the soprano part "O Star" in Randall Thompson's "Choose Something Like a Star," from *Frostiana* (Boston: E. C. Schirmer), 2487, SATB, Level 5.

STANDARD 6C

Listening to, analyzing, and describing music: Students identify and explain compositional devices and techniques used to provide unity and variety and tension and release in a musical work and give examples of other works that make similar uses of these devices and techniques.

Objective

- Students will identify and explain *cantus firmus* as a unifying device in Renaissance music.

Materials

- "Agnus Dei," from *Missa Dixit Maria,* by Hans Leo Hassler (Miami: Warner Bros. Publications), SV9007, SATB, Level 3; and "Dixit Maria," from *Missa Dixit Maria* (Miami: Warner Bros Publications), FEC 09679, SATB, Level 3; or any two works that are related by cantus firmus

Prior Knowledge and Experiences

- Students have been rehearsing the selected works.
- Students have experience identifying expressive devices in music.

Procedures

1. Tell students that as they sing or listen to "Agnus Dei" and "Dixit Maria," they should listen for what the two pieces have in common. Have students follow the scores, or sing the pieces, while you play them on the piano. Ask students what the two pieces have in common. After students have isolated the melodic figure, ask them to guess which piece was written later and based on the other one.

2. Define and explain cantus firmus as a melodic theme or subject. Ask students to speculate from where composers might have borrowed these melodies (e.g., chant, familiar melodies, folk songs, other composed works as in this example).

3. Ask the choir to sing measures 1–29 of "Agnus Dei," raising their hands when their section has the cantus firmus—or using the text or "tah" on the cantus firmus and "loo" on other material.

4. Help students discover imitative entrances with different starting pitches, slight variations in the cantus firmus melody, and the interplay of the supporting contrapuntal material that surrounds the cantus firmus. Emphasize how the cantus firmus is the unifying device and the other material provides contrast.

5. Have students listen to both compositions again and raise their hands when their section has the cantus firmus. Elicit from students comments about how unity and variety are created with the use of cantus firmus.

Indicators of Success

- Students define cantus firmus, explain its function as a unifying device, and identify examples of it visually and aurally.

Follow-up

- Give students other opportunities to hear a melodic theme or subject in a composed choral work and in its original source. Challenge them to examine the contrasting musical material and its relationship to the unity provided by the melodic theme.

Advanced

STANDARD 6D

Listening to, analyzing, and describing music: Students demonstrate the ability to perceive and remember music events by describing in detail significant events occurring in a given aural example.

Objective

- Students will identify aurally the fugue as a form, as well as the fugue subjects as they occur.

Materials

- "Sicut Locutus Est," from *Magnificat,* by Johann Sebastian Bach (New York: Carl Fischer), CM8111, SSATB, Level 4
- Recordings of "Sicut Locutus Est" and of other fugues, including choral (such as the closing chorus from Felix Mendelssohn's *Elijah*), orchestral (such as the overture from *Elijah*), and keyboard (such as Bach's *Well-Tempered Clavier*)
- Audio-playback equipment

Prior Knowledge and Experiences

- Students have studied the fugue as a musical form.
- Students can identify the "subject" as the main theme of the fugue.
- Students have been rehearsing "Sicut Locutus Est."

Procedures

1. Review the subject of the fugue in "Sicut Locutus Est" with students by having them sing it in unison and by referring to it as "the subject."
2. Play a recording of the piece and have students raise their hands when their sections sing the subject.
3. Sing the piece through, having sections stand when they sing the subject and sit when they have other material. If they have the work memorized, they should face the section that is singing the subject.
4. Introduce recordings of other fugues, playing each recording twice and challenging students to identify the subject and be able to sing it the first time. On the second playing, have them raise their hands to identify when they hear the fugue and in which voice or instrument it appears.

Indicators of Success

- Students identify a fugue when they hear one and identify the fugue's subject whenever it appears.

Follow-up

- Introduce other aspects of the typical fugue, such as stretto, episode, and countersubject. Explore the functions of these various aspects of fugue composition; for example, the tension in a stretto, the contrast provided by an episode, the typical way a countersubject contrasts with and complements the subject. Challenge students to identify these more subtle aspects of fugues in the fugue they are rehearsing and in others they hear.

STANDARD 6E

Listening to, analyzing, and describing music: Students compare ways in which musical materials are used in a given example relative to ways in which they are used in other works of the same genre or style.

Objective

- Students will compare two settings of the same text, from the Renaissance and the twentieth century, and identify their stylistic differences in the use of musical materials.

Materials

- "Resonet in Laudibus" by Jacob Handl (Fort Lauderdale, FL: Walton Music Corporation), W2151, SATB, Level 2; or another Renaissance choral work

- "Resonet in Laudibus" by Chester L. Alwes (Dayton, OH: The Lorenz Corporation), 10/1264R, SATB, Level 3; "Resonet in Laudibus" by Z. Randall Stroope (Champaign, IL: Mark Foster Music), MF553, SATB, Level 3; or another twentieth-century choral work using the same text as the selected Renaissance work

- Recordings of the selected pieces, as well as different settings of the same works from each of the two style periods

- Chalkboard

- Audio-playback equipment

Procedures

1. Review with students the meaning of the text in "Resonet in Laudibus" and then introduce the Handl setting, passing out the scores and then playing the recording of the work in its entirety.

2. After students have listened to the recording of the Renaissance setting of the piece several times, ask them to name the similarities as well as the differences in the Renaissance setting and the twentieth-century setting they have been rehearsing. Create two lists on the chalkboard. Guide students' listening to focus on all the elements of music (texture, harmony, dynamics, and so on) in their comparison. Help them, even in these early stages of analysis, to be specific in their comments and to use proper music vocabulary whenever possible.

3. Have students help you to further categorize their comments into new columns by elements: melody, harmony, texture, form, and so on. Lead students to keep refining their analytic comments, digging deeper to clarify specific stylistic aspects of the two pieces.

4. Help students to identify the broad stylistic differences (e.g., use of accompaniment vs. unaccompanied style, varieties of texture, variations in meter, use of dynamics) as well as more subtle ones (more angular, disjunct twentieth-century melody versus the smoother voice leading of the Renaissance; the dissonance of the twentieth century versus the controlled harmony of the Renaissance; different uses of the text).

5. Help students discover the similarities in stylistic approaches even though they may be subtle (e.g., the general jubilant spirit of each piece, which is achieved in different ways; Stroope's use of open fifths and descending triadic patterns, perhaps borrowed from the opening motive of the Handl). Through questioning and discussion, guide students to discover these aspects on their own.

6. Challenge students to apply what they are learning about these two styles to new listening examples of each. Play recorded excerpts and have students jot down ideas that will help them identify the style period of the unfamiliar work.

Prior Knowledge and Experiences

- Students can sing the selected twentieth-century choral work and understand the meaning of the text.
- Students have studied the elements of music.

Indicators of Success

- Students articulate general principles of choral music of the twentieth century versus the Renaissance.
- Students identify works from those periods when they hear them.

Follow-up

- Use a similar procedure with two works from the same style period, guiding students to discover more subtle differences and similarities.

STANDARD 6F

Listening to, analyzing, and describing music: Students analyze and describe uses of the elements of music in a given work that make it unique, interesting, and expressive.

Objective

- Students identify and describe the unique expressive aspects of a given choral work, applying their knowledge of compositional techniques.

Materials

- "David's Lamentation" by William Billings (Fort Lauderdale, FL: Walton Music Corporation), W2203, SATB, Level 2
- Chalkboard
- Student journals or portfolios

Prior Knowledge and Experiences

- Students can sing "David's Lamentation" competently.

Procedures

1. Review with students the definition of a chord (three or more notes sounding together). Have students sing through "David's Lamentation," stopping them on measure 8, 18, or 30. When they have stopped, ask them, "Is this a chord?" Help them to discover that these intervals are actually open fifths with no third.

2. Ask students how the open fifth sounds to them and how it makes them feel. Then discuss with them why Billings may have chosen that particular voicing in these places.

3. Ask students to check their scores for dynamic markings, and, at their direction, on the chalkboard make a ladder of dynamic markings in the piece from loudest to softest. Fill in the gaps on the ladder with other dynamics that are not used in the piece until there is a complete vertical chart from *fff* to *ppp*. Explain to students that these dynamics are not actually Billings's markings but rather those suggested by the editor. Then direct students to search for the softest dynamic. When they discover that the silence in measure 16 is the softest dynamic, explain that this dynamic is actually Billings's idea. Ask them to consider the effect of the one measure of silence. Give them an opportunity to share their own reactions to this dramatic moment.

4. Point out to students the unusual dotted rhythm in the tenor part in measure 2. Explain that because that rhythm appears only once in the piece, it must mean something, and ask students why they think Billings chose it. Let students share their ideas. Suggest the common tradition of using dotted rhythms in composing music for and about royalty.

5. Explain the phrase "text painting" as a device composers use to enhance the text; for example, a composer may write a descending octave interval when "painting" the text "heaven and earth." Let them find examples of text painting in the piece (perhaps the ascending melody on "went [up] to his chamber" or the triplet "sigh" in measure 28). Again, let students share their ideas and guide them to discover these aspects of the piece on their own.

6. Experiment with different tempos for the opening of the piece, probing students' imaginations for the "right" tempo and why they feel it is so. Discuss the characteristic long-short-short rhythm of the opening section and the steady beat feeling it sets up.

Suggest to students that Billings may be depicting David pacing slowly around his chamber. Have students walk around to the slow quarter notes as they sing, discovering a tempo that feels right.

7. Give students opportunities to express through writing (journal/portfolio) their feeling about the effectiveness and mood of these compositional choices, asking them, for example, "Which is your favorite way that Billing created the mood of grief in this piece? Why?"

Indicators of Success

- Students describe Billings's ideas and use of compositional techniques with correct vocabulary.

- Students draw connections between Billings's ideas and the overall mood they create.

Follow-up

- Have students compare the setting of "David's Lamentation" used in the procedures outlined above with another setting of the same text—for example, by G. S. Wilson (Milwaukee: G. Schirmer/Hal Leonard Corporation), 50312130, SATB, Level 3. Have students look for similarities of treatment or differences that reflect the composer's taste or style period aesthetics.

- Help students to draw connections between compositional craftsmanship and the unique, interesting, and expressive aspects of each piece they are rehearsing.

STANDARD 7A

Evaluating music and music performances: Students evolve specific criteria for making informed, critical evaluations of the quality and effectiveness of performances, compositions, arrangements, and improvisations and apply the criteria in their personal participation in music.

Objective

- Students will develop criteria for evaluating and choosing music, and help select appropriate literature for their own performance.

Materials

- Three to five recordings of potential works for the choir
- Scores for each recording
- Chalkboard
- Paper
- Audio-playback equipment

Prior Knowledge and Experiences

- Students have had experience in analyzing and discussing music.
- Students have studied the elements of music.
- Students have a sufficient vocabulary to describe musical events in a composition.
- Students have already performed at least one concert, giving them some basis for evaluating their ability.

Procedures

1. Lead a class discussion on the subject of choosing music for performance. Create two lists on the chalkboard to which students add their suggestions under the following headings: "What makes a good piece of music?" (e.g., effective use of text, tension and release, well-placed climaxes), and "What kinds of pieces would be good for our choir right now?" (e.g., no tenor divisi, more melismatic phrases, challenging harmonies).

2. Have students debate their ideas. Offer your input only to clarify and focus their suggestions. Encourage them to use what they already know about music and to use the most specific musical terms possible. Remind them to reflect especially on pieces that were most successful or "worked" well. Help them identify what vocal/technical problems need work, what strengths they possess, what repertoire will "balance their diet," and so on. Allow students to brainstorm freely.

3. From students' suggestions, write on the board and have them write on paper a rating system checklist that includes the titles of pieces to be considered and a space for written comments.

4. Play the selected recordings and have students follow along in the scores once without any written or verbal comments. The second time, give students time to write comments and evaluate the pieces.

5. Have students share their thoughts in a group discussion. Encourage students to defend their opinions logically and to weigh seriously the insights of their classmates. If possible, try to reach consensus about what repertoire to choose for the next concert.

Indicators of Success

- Students show careful consideration of the potential repertoire and defend their evaluations logically and thoughtfully.
- Students express their ideas using correct music vocabulary.

Follow-up

- Allow students to choose one of the selected pieces and develop a rehearsal strategy for how to begin learning it, including such things as possible warm-ups, where in the piece to begin rehearsing, and potential technical problems and how to deal with them.

Evaluating music and music performances: Students evolve specific criteria for making informed, critical evaluations of the quality and effectiveness of performances, compositions, arrangements, and improvisations and apply the criteria in their personal participation in music.

Objective

- Students will evaluate their own performance, identifying musical skills that need improvement, and develop specific musical exercises to address the problems.

Materials

- Choral work students have been rehearsing
- Audio-recording equipment, including stereo recorder, microphones, speakers, and blank tape
- Audio-playback equipment
- Rehearsal Critique Form (see example)
- Manuscript paper

Prior Knowledge and Experiences

- Students have discussed and practiced critical listening skills.
- Students have added critical listening terms (such as *intonation, blend,* and *tone quality*) to their vocabulary.
- Students have memorized a work in their repertoire, have listened to a professional recording of the work, and have discussed its style and various musical elements.

Procedures

1. Have students sing the work they have memorized while you record them.
2. Give each student a Rehearsal Critique Form (see example). Read through the form with them and discuss the various questions.
3. Have students follow their music as you play the recording of their singing. Then ask them to fill out the critique form through question 2 to evaluate their performance. Note particularly that, for question 2, they should focus on one specific area that needs improvement.
4. After students have completed questions 1 and 2 on the critique form, lead a class discussion on the types of warm-ups that could be used to address different problem areas students have identified. Then have students work on question 3 individually, using manuscript paper, if necessary.
5. Have students discuss and compare their evaluations. Ask volunteers for their remedial warm-up activity or vocalise, explaining the activity step by step.

Indicators of Success

- Students identify and critique their own performance strengths and weaknesses.
- Students create warm-up activities or vocalises to work on problem areas.

Follow-up

- Use student-generated vocal exercises in subsequent rehearsals to improve identified problems and weak areas.

- Students have developed specific criteria for evaluating their performances.

Rehearsal Critique Form

Name _____   Date _____

Voice Part _____   Class _____

Selection being rehearsed _____

****

1. Identify one specific place in the music or one aspect of our performance that seems particularly strong to you and explain why.

2. Identify one specific aspect of the music that needs to be improved (e.g., intonation, blend, tone quality, or rhythmic accuracy). Be specific and include the page number and measure number. For example: "My section can improve the intonation on page 2 in measure 12," or "I need to . . . on . . . "

3. Develop a remedial warm-up activity or vocalise to address this problem. Explain the activity step by step.

STANDARD 7A

Evaluating music and music performances: Students evolve specific criteria for making informed, critical evaluations of the quality and effectiveness of performances, compositions, arrangements, and improvisations and apply the criteria in their personal participation in music.

Objective

- Students will observe and evaluate their own rehearsal.

Materials

- Choral works to be rehearsed
- Rehearsal Observation Form (see example)

Prior Knowledge and Experiences

- Students have been practicing listening and analysis skills and have discussed criteria for evaluating their performances.
- Students can define and explain terms such as *vocal technique, blend, balance,* and *tone.*
- Students can take simple melodic dictation.

Procedures

1. Ask a student from each section to sit out and not participate in singing during the rehearsal. Then give each student in the class the Rehearsal Observation Form. Explain that students who sit out of the rehearsal will use the form to record a summary of what they see and hear, including notating vocalises, and make suggestions for improvement.

2. Place students who are going to sit out of rehearsal where they can observe the entire rehearsal. Continue with a normal rehearsal, stopping ten minutes before the end of class.

3. Have observers share some of the comments from their forms with the class.

Indicators of Success

- Students accurately describe what they see and hear (including notating vocalises that are sung), evaluate the rehearsal, and provide suggestions for the next rehearsal, all using appropriate terminology.

Follow-up

- Have different students observe each day or once a week, and use student critiques to plan future rehearsals. Save these forms so that over the course of the rehearsal process, progress can be noted. For example, quoting a student evaluation from early in the rehearsal process several weeks later will encourage students about their progress.

Rehearsal Observation Form

Name _____ Date _____

The reason I sat out from rehearsal today is _____

I. The physical/mental warm-up used today was _____

II. The vocal warm-ups used today were the following:

A. The first vocalise:

_____

_____

_____

_____

The purpose of this vocalise was to _____

The problems I heard or observations I made during this vocalise were _____

_____

B. The second vocalise:

_____

_____

_____

_____

The purpose of this vocalise was to _____

The problems I heard or observations I made during this vocalise were _____

_____

C. Other observations I made during the warm-up (regarding Vocal Technique, Posture, Blend, Balance, Tone, and so on) were _____

_____

III. What was rehearsed?

A. The first selection rehearsed was (name piece and composer) _____

Measure numbers rehearsed were _____

The goal of this rehearsal was to _____

(Check one of the following and answer the accompanying question.)

___ The choir did achieve that goal by _____

___ The choir did not achieve that goal because _____

B. The second selection rehearsed was (name piece and composer) _____

Measure numbers rehearsed were _____

The goal of this rehearsal was to _____

(Check one of the following and answer the accompanying question.)

___ The choir did achieve that goal by _____

___ The choir did not achieve that goal because _____

IV. Summary

Were there any surprises or new insights you gained from listening today? _____

What suggestions do you have for tomorrow's rehearsal? _____

Evaluating music and music performances: Students evaluate a performance, composition, arrangement, or improvisation by comparing it to similar or exemplary models.

Objective

- Students will critically evaluate a musical performance by a group other than their own, comparing it to what they envision to be an exemplary performance of the work.

Materials

- Copies of two or more musical reviews of the same performance by different critics
- Choir Comment Form (see example)
- Selected recording of a choral performance
- Audio-playback equipment

Prior Knowledge and Experiences

- Students have developed critical listening, analysis, and evaluation skills.
- Students have studied the elements of music and have a sufficient vocabulary to describe music they hear.
- Students have had the opportunity to question a music critic (perhaps someone who freelances for the local paper) and learn how a critic prepares for a performance, discover some basic strategies for evaluating a performance, and gain insights into this kind of writing.

Procedures

1. Review with students what they learned from the music critic about what to listen for when evaluating a performance. Discuss with them what they learned about the differences between critiquing a performance and describing and critiquing the music itself.

2. Give students copies of two or more reviews of the same performance. Help them see how aspects of writing style (such as point of view and tone) affect the reader's impression of the performance. [*Note:* For additional ideas, refer to the book *Making Sense: Teaching Critical Reading Across the Curriculum,* edited by Anne Chapman (New York: College Entrance Examination Board, 1993).]

3. Provide students with a copy of the Choir Comment Form or a similar form that the class has created. Play the selected recording and, asking them to use what they have learned about critiquing performances, have students write a one-to-two-page review comparing the performance on the recording to what they would envision to be a "perfect," or exemplary, performance of the work. Explain that they should use the form you distributed as a checklist and mental organizer in critiquing the performance and use appropriate music vocabulary.

Indicators of Success

- Students apply the criteria from the Choir Comment Form and effectively compare the recorded performance to what they envision to be an exemplary performance of the work.
- Students use appropriate music vocabulary in their written reviews.

Follow-up

- Arrange for students to attend a performance individually or as a group. Ask them to write a two-to-four-page review, using what they have learned about critiquing performances.

Choir Comment Form

Wisconsin School Music Association

For Student Use Only

Student Name: _____

Performing Choir: _____

Selection Titles or Number: _____

TONE

_____

❏ Good Support ❏ Lack Support ❏ Vibrato is Appropriate ❏ Vibrato is Inappropriate
❏ Voices Blend Well ❏ Voices Do Not Blend ❏ Free, Full, Rounded Tone ❏ Thin or Breathy Tone

Comments: _____

INTONATION

	In Tune	Out of Tune		In Tune	Out of Tune
Within Sections	❏	❏	Inner Parts	❏	❏
Melody	❏	❏	Chords	❏	❏

Comments: _____

BALANCE

❏ All Parts Balanced   ❏ All Sections Heard
❏ S ❏ A ❏ T ❏ B Section Overpowers   ❏ S ❏ A ❏ T ❏ B Section Not Heard

Comments: _____

TECHNIQUE

❏ Adequate Breath Support ❏ Inadequate Breath Support ❏ Good Precision ❏ Poor Precision
❏ Pitches Not Accurate ❏ Pitches Were Right On ❏ Good Posture ❏ Poor Posture
❏ Entrances & Releases Together ❏ Entrances & Releases Not Together

Comments: _____

INTERPRETATION & MUSICAL EFFECT

❏ Mood was Effective   ❏ Mood was not Reflected in Singing or Body Language
❏ Dynamic Contrast Evident   ❏ Dynamic Contrast Not Evident
❏ Phrasing Well Done   ❏ Phrasing Not Appropriate to Text
❏ Tempo Was Appropriate   ❏ Tempo Not Appropriate

Comments: _____

DICTION

❏ Open Mouths & Pure Vowel Sounds   ❏ Vowels Sound Pinched or Tight
❏ Consonants Clear and Energetic   ❏ Consonants Need Emphasis

Comments: _____

OTHER FACTORS:

Comment on Stage Presence, Energy, Facial Expression, Following the Director, Music Selection.

_____

_____

_____

Most impressive aspect of this performance:_____

Area that seems to need improvement:_____

STANDARD 7B
STRATEGY 2 OF 2

Evaluating music and music performances: Students evaluate a performance, composition, arrangement, or improvisation by comparing it to similar or exemplary models.

Objective

- Students will write a review of a choral festival performance, comparing it to their own performance of a specific piece by exploring the role of the festival adjudicator.

Materials

- Chalkboard
- Copies of several adjudicators' comment sheets for a given performance by another choral ensemble that performed the selected work that the choir has been rehearsing
- Choir Comment Form (see previous strategy)
- Audio-playback equipment

Other Requirements

- Choral director/adjudicator (from a local church or college)

Prior Knowledge and Experiences

- Students have been developing critical listening, analysis, and evaluation skills.
- Students have studied the elements of music and have a sufficient vocabulary to describe music they hear.

Procedures

1. Discuss with students what they think specifically an adjudicator listens for when evaluating a performance. Write students' suggestions on the chalkboard.

2. Introduce the choral director or adjudicator and ask this person to share some basic strategies for evaluating a performance. Ask him or her to help students clarify the differences between critiquing a performance and describing and critiquing the music itself. Allow students to spend ten minutes asking the choral director or adjudicator the questions they have prepared.

3. Give students copies of several reviews from the same performance. (These could be obtained through cooperative efforts with the conductor of the given choral ensemble.) Help students see how both musical factors (e.g., tone, diction, blend, balance, appropriateness to style) as well as nonmusical factors (e.g., entrance and exit from stage, facial expressions and body language, behavior between selections, attentiveness to concert attire) affect the adjudicator's impression of the performance. Note that most adjudicators make references to both factors in their comments.

4. Play the students' performance of the selected work and invite students to take notes on the Choir Comment Form.

5. Ask students to write a one-to-two-page review comparing the choral festival performance they heard earlier and their own recorded performance, using what they have learned about critiquing performances.

Indicators of Success

- Students write reviews that logically compare the festival performance of a given choir with their own performance, using musical terminology.

- Students have attended a festival in which the selected work was performed and used the Choir Comment Form to take notes.

- Students have recorded their performance of the selected work during a previous rehearsal.

- Students have prepared questions for the visiting choral director or adjudicator. Their questions should deal with aspects of the choral director or adjudicator's job or ways in which he or she analyzes a performance.

Follow-up

- Have students write critical comments of their own performances in concerts and festivals by listening and responding to recordings of the given performance. [*Note:* This could be especially fruitful following a performance in a choral festival if done before the adjudicator's comments are read and discussed with the choir. Students could then compare their evaluations with those of the adjudicators.]

STANDARD 7C

Evaluating music and music performances: Students evaluate a given musical work in terms of its aesthetic qualities and explain the musical means it uses to evoke feelings and emotions.

Objective

- Students will evaluate a choral work by examining the aesthetic choices the composer made to evoke emotion.

Materials

- "Peaceful Vale" ("Ruhetal" or "Valley of Rest") by Felix Mendelssohn, arr. Frank Mueller (Van Nuys, CA: Alfred Publishing Company), 04-70603, SATB, Level 3 [*Note:* When performing translations, be certain to refer to the original text so that the musical elements match the text accurately.]

Prior Knowledge and Experiences

- Students have discussed the text of "Peaceful Vale," a translation of the original German text.

Procedures

1. Have students read through the text of "Peaceful Vale" to themselves and reflect upon all they have discussed over the previous rehearsals.

2. Ask students to sing through the piece, giving careful consideration to the technical aspects of the music they have discussed.

3. Lead a discussion on the many aspects of Mendelssohn's compositional style and specific choices he made in "Peaceful Vale." Ask students which of Mendelssohn's musical ideas are most effective for them and when their favorite moment in the piece occurs.

4. When students have all shared their individual thoughts, help them discover whether all of their thoughts lead them to a description of "Peaceful Vale."

5. Have students sing through the piece again, this time focusing on the expression of the whole composition. Guide them in demonstrating the relationship between the technical and the textual aspects of the piece.

Indicators of Success

- Students describe how specific musical elements of "Peaceful Vale" match with the text.

- Students use appropriate vocabulary in their explanations of how the composer evokes feelings and emotions.

Follow-up

- Invite students to think of their favorite special place as they sing "Peaceful Vale" during a subsequent rehearsal. Give them a chance to reflect on the piece in their journals.

- Students have analyzed various technical aspects of "Peaceful Vale" and their contribution to Mendelssohn's style and intent; for example: the opening pedal point, the text painting, and the use of repetition and contrast in melodic and harmonic materials.

- Students have learned appropriate music vocabulary to discuss the technical aspects of the work.

- Students can sing "Peaceful Vale" competently.

STANDARD 8A

Understanding relationships between music, the other arts, and disciplines outside the arts: Students explain how elements, artistic processes, and organizational principles are used in similar and distinctive ways in the various arts and cite examples.

Objective

■ Students will identify and relate the musical ABA form with ABA form in visual art and architecture, and they will explain the reasons for the prevalence of ABA form in the arts.

Materials

■ Chalkboard

■ Pictures of ABA form in architecture and visual art (e.g., the Capitol in Washington, D.C., Notre Dame Cathedral, Sacred Heart Basilica, *Adoration of the Magi* by Botticelli, *The Declaration of Independence* by Trumbull)

Prior Knowledge and Experiences

■ Students have identified the ABA structure of a piece they are rehearsing.

Procedures

1. Review with students the ABA form of the piece they have been rehearsing. Explain that ABA form is very common in the arts, and ask them to ponder the reasons for this phenomenon. Allow students to share their insights. Guide them to consider ABA form in nature and let them think of examples (e.g., eye-nose-eye or ear-mouth-ear).

2. Show students pictures of ABA form in architecture. If they have trouble seeing the form, break it down into simple line drawings for them. Ask them to name local buildings that are in ABA form.

3. Show students pictures of paintings in ABA form. Point out the form if it is unclear to students.

4. Ask students again why they think that ABA form is so common in visual art, architecture, and music. Allow them to discuss the principles of unity (the two As, the return of A, the feeling of closure, the importance of familiarity, etc.) versus contrast (A versus B, the importance of variety to prevent boredom, etc.). While they are discussing these principles, guide them with questions such as, "What would you think of a musical work in the form AAAA? What about ABCDEF?"

Indicators of Success

■ Students identify ABA form in music, visual art, and architecture when they see or hear it.

■ Students describe the advantages of ABA form as an organizational principle in the arts.

Follow-up

■ Invite students to categorize other buildings, artworks, and pieces of music by form (e.g., AB, ABBA, ABC). Take the class outside to the front of the school to determine its structure.

Understanding relationships between music, the other arts, and disciplines outside the arts: Students compare characteristics of two or more arts within a particular historical period or style and cite examples from various cultures.

Objective

- Students will compare examples of music and visual art from the Baroque period and identify similar characteristics in their style.

Materials

- Reproduction of Baroque ceiling painting *The Entrance of St. Ignatius into Paradise* by Fra Andrea Pozzo, or *The Glorification of the Reign of Urban VIII* by Cortona

- Reproduction of Baroque painting *Judith and Maidservant* by Gentileschi, or *The Conversion of St. Paul* by Caravaggio

Prior Knowledge and Experiences

- Students have been rehearsing "For unto Us a Child Is Born," from *Messiah,* by George Frideric Handel (New York: Carl Fischer), 50294190, SATB, Level 5; or another exemplary chorus with typical Baroque features.

- Students have been introduced to the term *Baroque.*

Procedures

1. Show students the reproduction of a very ornate Baroque ceiling painting. Ask them when they think the painting was created and have them explain their answers. Discuss with students various aspects of the painting, focusing their attention on the "busy," ornate style and the overwhelming effect of the painting.

2. Ask students what aspects of the Handel work they have been singing are similar to the painting they just discussed. Help students to recognize the excessive, dramatic repetition of a relatively short text, the elaborate melismas, and so on. Explain that these aspects of art are characteristics that define Baroque style.

3. Show students the Gentileschi or Caravaggio painting. Ask them what the most outstanding characteristic of the painting is and help them to focus on the extreme contrast in light and dark. Explain to students that extreme contrast is an important aspect of Baroque art.

4. Ask students to pick out the extreme contrast in the Handel chorus (i.e., contrasts in dynamics, such as the "Wonderful, Counselor" section versus the melismatic sections).

5. Have students sing through the Handel piece, keeping in mind the Baroque characteristics they have discussed.

Indicators of Success

- Students identify characteristics of Baroque style in unfamiliar examples of visual art and relate those characteristics to music they are singing.

- Students describe the characteristics of Baroque music using appropriate music vocabulary.

Follow-up

- Choose artworks that represent other aspects of Baroque style and relate them to the Baroque music the students are learning; for example, have students compare rhythm and movement in a sculpture such as Bernini's *David* or a painting such as Rubens's *The Raising of the Cross* with the insistent, driving rhythm of a selected Handel piece.

STANDARD 8B

Understanding relationships between music, the other arts, and disciplines outside the arts: Students compare characteristics of two or more arts within a particular historical period or style and cite examples from various cultures.

Objective

- Students will identify and compare three features of Japanese visual art and music: the principle of understatement, the attention to form and formalism, and the emphasis on nature themes.

Materials

- "Sakura," a Japanese folk song, arr. Linda Steen Spevacek (Milwaukee: Hal Leonard Corporation), 08756912, two-part, Level 3

- Prints or photographs of Japanese landscape paintings, screens, or woodblock prints

- Photographs of Japanese Zen gardens

- Recording of "Variations on Sakura," on *Art of the Koto: The Music of Japan Played by Kimia Eto,* Elektra Records CD 70234

- Audio-playback equipment

- Chalkboard

Prior Knowledge and Experiences

- Students have been rehearsing "Sakura."

- Students are familiar with the term *texture*.

Procedures

1. Have students sing through "Sakura." Ask them whether the textures in the piece are relatively thick or thin. When they conclude that the textures are thin, ask them how thin textures in music translate to thin textures in visual art (e.g., few lines, delicate strokes, muted colors).

2. Show students a delicately textured Japanese landscape, nature painting, or woodblock print. Let them discuss the similarities in style between what they see and the textures of "Sakura."

3. Show students several more examples of Japanese art and lead them to discover the common nature theme as a characteristic of Japanese art.

4. Show students a photo of a Zen garden and ask them what kind of mood is created by the garden. Discuss with them the Zen influence of beauty, quiet, and peace as an aesthetic. Point out the formal aspect of the garden and the Japanese emphasis on form and formalism in general in writing *kanji* (the Chinese characters that were adopted into the Japanese writing system), folding paper for origami, and the ritual of the tea ceremony.

5. Play the recording of "Variations on Sakura" for students. On the chalkboard, create a call chart, listing the sections and a breakdown by measures, to help them focus on the theme with three variations. Discuss with them the delicate texture of the piece and ask them to compare it to other pieces in their repertoire. Help them discover the traditional Japanese aesthetic of understatement or "less is more."

6. Have students sing once again, keeping in mind what they have learned about Japanese art and texture.

Indicators of Success

- Students summarize several features of Japanese art, using appropriate vocabulary, and relate these features to music they sing and hear.

Follow-up

- Invite students to bring in other examples of various forms of Japanese art or music. Let the class analyze and describe each work. Encourage them to use specific vocabulary and to examine each work afresh.

- Introduce students to other aspects of Japanese culture (e.g., cuisine, traditional dress, architecture) and draw parallels where possible to artistic principles already studied.

- Give students opportunities to hear examples of Japanese music. For resources, see *Multicultural Perspectives in Music Education,* 2d ed., by William Anderson and Patricia Shehan Campbell (Reston, VA: Music Educators National Conference, 1996).

STANDARD 8C

Understanding relationships between music, the other arts, and disciplines outside the arts:
Students explain ways in which the principles and subject matter of various disciplines
outside the arts are interrelated with those of music.

Objective

- Students will discover relationships between opera and literature and be able to explain these interrelationships.

Materials

- Short novel, play, or short story that students have read for another class. [*Note:* You may want to consult students' literature teacher to choose an appropriate piece of literature and teach this strategy cooperatively.]

Prior Knowledge and Experiences

- Students have seen a live opera or opera excerpts on video.
- Students are familiar with operatic forms (overture, aria, recitative, ensemble, chorus, entr'acte, and so on) and their function in the typical opera structure.
- Students have read the selected literature.

Procedures

1. Review with students the characters and plot in the selected piece of literature.

2. Have students brainstorm about the kinds of things they would need to consider in adapting the work as an opera. List their ideas on the chalkboard. These should include considerations such as characters, voice parts of characters, musical features and styles for each character, adaptation of the story itself, elimination of sections of the story, division of the work into scenes and acts, dialogue, arias and who sings them.

3. Ask students to consider questions such as the following:

   - Which characters will be featured and which eliminated? What voice parts will the characters be and why? What particular musical features and styles will the music have for each character? How will musical characterization be achieved?

   - How will the story itself be adapted for the stage? Which sections of the story could be eliminated? How will the work be broken into scenes and acts?

   - What sections of dialogue will become recitative-style singing? Where will the arias be and who will sing them?

   - What kinds of ensembles (duets, trios, etc.) will you use and where? Will you use a chorus in your drama? How and where?

   - What part will the orchestra play in the dramatic structure of your work? Will you use an overture or interludes, and what kind of moods will they convey? Will you use a standard orchestra or a chamber-sized group? All traditional instruments or other additional ones?

4. Based on the discussion, ask students to speculate on how well this work will translate to opera. Ask them to explain their reasoning.

5. Have students describe the interrelationship between opera and literature. Guide them in recognizing the role of the composer in choosing a specific direction.

Indicators of Success

- Students demonstrate their understanding of the relationships between literature and opera.
- Students identify the unique characteristics of opera form.

Follow-up

- Have each student choose a section of the selected text that they would adapt as an aria and then create the actual aria text, describing musically how they would adapt it for the opera. This could include actual melodic composition of themes, motives, and so on, depending on the ability level of students.
- Give students a long-term assignment to create a logical, imaginative, and thoughtful opera scenario based on the questions in the procedures outlined above.

Understanding relationships between music, the other arts, and disciplines outside the arts: Students compare the uses of characteristic elements, artistic processes, and organizational principles among the arts in different historical periods and different cultures.

Objective

- Students will identify pointillism in visual art and compare it with "musical pointillism."

Materials

- "Sunday," from *Sunday in the Park with George* by Stephen Sondheim (Miami: Warner Bros. Publications), VAL2018, vocal selections
- Text of "Sunday"
- Recording of Stephen Sondheim's *Sunday in the Park with George,* RCA RCD1-5042
- Reproduction of *Sunday Afternoon on the Island of La Grande Jatte,* by Georges Seurat, in *Music! Its Role and Importance in Our Lives* by Charles Fowler (New York: Glencoe/McGraw-Hill, 1994)
- Chalkboard
- Audio-playback equipment

Prior Knowledge and Experiences

- None required.

Procedures

1. Ask students to study the painting *Sunday Afternoon on the Island of La Grande Jatte,* allowing them to discover and discuss unique aspects of this painting style.

2. Lead students to understand pointillism as a post-Impressionist phenomenon. Help them to notice the outdoor setting, intense colors, and bright sunlight of the painting (all characteristics shared with Impressionism) and the dots of color that create a shimmering, mosaic-like effect. Write a definition of "pointillism" on the chalkboard. Explain to students that the painting was the inspiration for the music to *Sunday in the Park with George.*

3. Ask students to describe how they would create pointillism in music. List their suggestions on the chalkboard.

4. Give students a copy of the text of "Sunday" and have them review it for what they might consider to be the pointillistic effects. Record their responses on the chalkboard. Discuss George's first four words ("design, tension, balance, harmony") with regard to both the painting and the text of the song.

5. From the recording, play "Sunday" (the first minute and twenty seconds) or "Color and Light" and have students identify the similarities between the music and the painting (e.g., "dots" of musical color). List these similarities on the chalkboard.

6. Play the recording of "Sunday" (especially the instrumental scoring under the opening dialogue), asking students to listen for the pointillistic effects. Then have them summarize how those effects were achieved.

Indicators of Success

- Students define pointillism, describe it within its historical perspective, and compare its use in music and visual art.

Follow-up

- Show students the portion of the videotape *Ferris Bueller's Day Off* (Hollywood: Paramount Home Video, 1996) in which students visit the museum and view the painting *Sunday Afternoon on the Island of La Grande Jatte.*

- Provide opportunities for students to listen to other music inspired by paintings, such as Mussorgsky's *Pictures at an Exhibition* or Allen Shearer's "Nude Descending a Staircase," on *Out of This World,* Chanticleer, Joseph Jennings, Teldec 4509-96515-2.

- Introduce students to another highly specific use of color in music—the *Klangfarbenmelodie* ("tone color melody") of Arnold Schoenberg and Anton Webern. Some good examples of this tone color melody are Schoenberg's *Five Pieces for Orchestra,* op. 16, 3d movement, and Webern's Symphony, op. 21.

Understanding relationships between music, the other arts, and disciplines outside the arts: Students compare the uses of characteristic elements, artistic processes, and organizational principles among the arts in different historical periods and different cultures.

Objective

■ Students will describe differences between the aesthetics of Romanticism and Classicism.

Materials

■ "Where Are You?" worksheets (see example)

■ Choral work from the Romantic period

■ Choral work from the Classical period

Prior Knowledge and Experiences

■ Students have begun rehearsing the selected Romantic and Classical choral works.

Procedures

1. Distribute the "Where Are You?" worksheets and ask students to put an X along the continuum at the point that best describes themselves. Ask, for example, "Are you 'logical' or 'illogical' or somewhere in the middle?"

2. When students have completed the worksheets, ask them to "show" where they marked themselves by standing as a group along a line in the classroom or gymnasium. Announce which end of the line is the word at one end of the continuum, and have students position themselves accordingly.

3. Lead a brief discussion about students' reaction to the experience. "Did you find yourself mostly checking one side of the sheet? How many checked mostly to the right? To the left? Were you surprised at some things you saw? Any new insights?"

4. Explain to students the historical polarity in the arts between Romanticism (generally the characteristics on the right) and Classicism (the left). Note that throughout history there has been a pendulum constantly swinging back and forth between these two extremes of artistic values. Explain that through their study of these two style periods, they will be exploring the two philosophies and seeing how they influenced composers, writers, and artists. Tell them, "By the time we're through, you should be able to define yourself as primarily a Romanticist or Classicist or a mixture of both, and explain why."

5. As a beginning activity in this process of exploration, ask students to sing through the Classical piece and the Romantic piece that they have been rehearsing. Based on the activity they completed with the worksheets, have them brainstorm about some of the characteristics that distinguish these two pieces. List these characteristics on the chalkboard, relating them to the personality characteristics they have discussed. To help them fine-tune the list on the chalkboard, remind them of other works that they have sung from these two style periods.

Indicators of Success

■ Students define some general characteristics of Classicism and Romanticism.

■ Students identify characteristics of these two style periods in music they are rehearsing.

Follow-up

■ Continue to explore both the Classical and Romantic aesthetic philosophies as students rehearse representative music from the style periods. Use examples from visual art, poetry, and architecture, and have students compare and contrast the characteristics of the Classical and Romantic artworks and relate them to what they know about representative music of the periods.

"Where Are You?"

logical. . . . . illogical

reserved. . . . . passionate

cool, calm. . . . . temperamental

practical. . . . . imaginative

sophisticated. . . . . down-to-earth

organized. . . . . messy

shy. . . . . expressive

realistic. . . . . idealistic

closed. . . . . open

tame. . . . . wild

conservative. . . . . risk-taking

Understanding relationships between music, the other arts, and disciplines outside the arts: Students explain how the roles of creators, performers, and others involved in the production and presentation of the arts are similar to and different from one another in the various arts.

Objective

- Students will describe the various roles involved in producing a professional musical theatre production.

Materials

- Student worksheets (teacher generated)—see step 1
- Video recording *Broadway Backstage!* (The Midtown Management Group, Inc., 120 West 44th Street, Suite 601, New York, NY 10036; telephone 212-398-6740), 1985
- Videocassette recorder
- Video monitor
- Chalkboard

Prior Knowledge and Experiences

- None required

Procedures

1. Distribute a worksheet that includes columns headed Jobs Onstage, Jobs Offstage, and Job Description to guide students' viewing of *Broadway Backstage.* Inform students that they may also write down new terms they hear—and list them in a fourth column—as they watch the video.

2. Have students watch and take notes as you play the video.

3. Discuss the various jobs involved in musical theatre productions: composer, lyricist, bookwriter, choreographer, instrumentalist, actor, costumer, director, and so on. On the chalkboard, set up two columns: Music and Theatre. Ask students to tell you which jobs to write under which columns.

4. Test students' understanding of these jobs by having them explain which are similar in both music and theatre and which are specific to just one or the other.

5. Have students write on their forms a comparison between one offstage and one onstage job, noting the relationship between these two roles (e.g., the relationship of costumer and actor or composer and conductor).

Indicators of Success

- Students identify the jobs needed to produce a musical theatre production and explain their interrelationship using appropriate vocabulary.

Follow-up

- If students are in the middle of rehearsing their own show, pause occasionally and ask, "Who wrote this lyric? This line? Whose job would that be?" Identify the historical persons associated with the show they are rehearsing and let them research the collaborative process, the ups and downs, and the production history of their show.

STANDARD 8E

Understanding relationships between music, the other arts, and disciplines outside the arts: Students explain how the roles of creators, performers, and others involved in the production and presentation of the arts are similar to and different from one another in the various arts.

Objective

■ Students describe the role of a composer, identify how the background of a composer may influence his or her work, and compare the composer's role to that of a visual artist.

Materials

■ Copies of letter students have received from composer

Prior Knowledge and Experiences

■ Students have been rehearsing a choral work by a living composer.

■ Students have written to and received a response from the composer whose work they have been rehearsing. Their letter to the composer included questions about the construction and compositional history of the choral work being rehearsed and other details of interest to them about the work. [*Note:* Composer's address may be secured through the publisher, or you may send the letter in care of the publisher, perhaps first making a contact with an editor who will forward the letter for you.]

Procedures

1. Distribute the copies of the composer's letter to students. Give students a chance to read it silently. Then discuss with students the composer's responses to questions such as the following:

   ■ Where did you get the idea for this piece?

   ■ What attracted you to the text?

   ■ What was the first musical theme or idea you had?

   ■ Where did you begin in the compositional process?

   ■ Which part of the piece was finished first? How long did it take to write? Which part was particularly difficult to finish?

   ■ What aspect of the piece is most satisfying for you?

   ■ Do you compose as a full-time job? How did you get started?

2. Re-examine with students the composer's work that they have been rehearsing. Ask them how the composer's insights affect their understanding of the work. Discuss with them how it will affect their interpretation or appreciation of the work.

3. Help students assemble the information into a meaningful understanding of the composer's personal background and its relationship to the music being studied. Guide them to describe the role of the composer and how it relates to their role as performers. Elicit from students how a visual artist's role is similar or different from that of a composer.

4. Based on what they have learned about the composer, have students write program notes for their concert program.

Indicators of Success

■ Students discuss and articulate aspects of a composer's personal background and his or her music and the interrelationship of both.

■ Students describe the role of the composer and relate it to their own role as performers.

■ Students cite similarities and differences in the roles of the composer and the visual artist.

(continued)

Follow-up

- If the composer lives nearby, invite him or her to speak to the class. Also consider inviting the composer to the students' performance of the work.

- Use the program notes students have written for the concert program, and perhaps have students share what they have learned about the composer in a verbal presentation for the audience. Have a student enlarge and mount the composer's letter, along with the letter to the composer and other materials that relate to the composer's life and work. Display these in the halls on the night of the performance.

Proficient

STANDARD 9A

Understanding music in relation to history and culture: *Students classify by genre or style and by historical period or culture unfamiliar but representative aural examples of music and explain the reasoning behind their classifications.*

Objective

- Students will define the term *style* in music and identify the style period of selected excerpts.

Materials

- Recorded excerpts of many musical styles and genres
- "How Old?" worksheet (see step 1)
- Audio-playback equipment
- Chalkboard

Prior Knowledge and Experiences

- Students have studied the elements of music.
- Students understand the terms *dissonance* and *texture*.

Procedures

1. Distribute the "How Old?" worksheet, which includes columns headed "Very Old," "Old," and "Fairly New." Inform students that you are going to play several excerpts of works of various musical styles and genres and that they should use the elements of music to focus their listening. Play the excerpts and, after each excerpt, have students mark an X under the appropriate column and write down a few reasons for their choice, using appropriate music vocabulary.

2. Play the excerpts again, stopping after each one to discuss students' answers and the reasons for their responses. In the discussion, encourage students to place each excerpt in the context of what they may know about history. Always ask them to justify their response more specifically than "It just sounds like it."

3. Introduce students to the idea of style by defining musical style as the distinctive or characteristic manner in which the elements of music are treated. Explain that there are a number of clues they can use to identify the style of a piece. Using dissonance as an example, help students deduce that newer music is often more complex from a harmonic standpoint, and that listening for dissonance is one good way to place music in its proper historical period. Then you might use texture as an example, explaining that as harmonies have grown more complex throughout history, so has the use of texture, especially in orchestral works.

4. Have students listen to recorded excerpts illustrating the examples used in step 3. Ask students to identify which of two excerpts is from a later style period.

5. Introduce the names of the style periods (e.g., Baroque, Classical), listing them on the chalkboard with their approximate dates. Focus on one or two style periods, and have students listen for one or two elements to help them hear the distinct styles. For example, help students identify the long, spinning, asymmetrical and very ornamented melodies of the Baroque by comparing them with the much simpler, generally asymmetrical, and logical Classical melodies.

6. Play another excerpt from one of the style periods used in step 5, asking students to identify the style period and explain their choice.

(continued)

7. Conclude by summarizing with students how the elements of music are used in distinctive ways to create different musical styles.

Indicators of Success

- Students make logical choices and use appropriate music vocabulary in identifying the age and style period for selected musical excerpts.

- Students use their knowledge of the elements of music in classifying music by age and style period.

Follow-up

- Introduce the characteristics of each musical style period and, as students refine their listening skills, play "drop the needle" until they can differentiate style periods with regularity.

STANDARD 9B

Understanding music in relation to history and culture: Students identify sources of American music genres, trace the evolution of those genres, and cite well-known musicians associated with them.

Objective

- Students will aurally identify American pop songs and jazz standards and compare versions of a song performed in each genre.

Materials

- Recordings of "My Funny Valentine," performed by Tony Bennett on *The American Popular Song Collection,* disc 5, Smithsonian CD RP0006; performed by Ella Fitzgerald, on *The Rodgers & Hart Songbook,* vol. 2, Verve 821579-2; and performed by Sarah Vaughan, on *The Smithsonian Collection of Classic Jazz,* disc 4, Smithsonian RJ0010

- "My Funny Valentine" (refrain melody and text), in *Music! Its Role and Importance in Our Lives,* by Charles Fowler (New York: Glencoe/McGraw-Hill, 1994)

- Broadway, pop, and jazz versions of another American standard song

- Audio-playback equipment

Prior Knowledge and Experiences

- Students have sung "My Funny Valentine" in unison.

Procedures

1. From the text, have students sing "My Funny Valentine." Briefly discuss with them the structure of the piece (AA'BA'' tag), its use of motivic repetition, and its emotional high point and how it is achieved.

2. Ask students whether they know where or how the song originated (Broadway show, *Babes in Arms*). Discuss with students how early popular songs originated in Broadway shows.

3. Play the Tony Bennett recording. Ask students to guess when it was recorded [1959] and in what genre [pop song]. Ask students how the recorded version differs from what they have been singing. [Verse begins the recorded version.] Explain the standard verse-chorus structure of the 32-bar song form—four sections of eight bars each, in an AABA pattern.

4. Ask students to surmise what the advantages might be for singers in using just piano for accompaniment. Help students understand the natural progression from hit show song to hit pop song, pointing out how pop songs became popular in 1959.

5. Play the Ella Fitzgerald recording. See if students can guess who the singer is. If not, inform them, and compare it with the previous recording: Help students to hear the similarities [the use of full orchestra] and the differences [Fitzgerald has a considerably more jazz-oriented vocal style] between the two recordings. Ask students what makes Ella Fitzgerald's a more jazz-flavored recording [tone quality, bending and substituting pitches, singing almost always a little behind the beat, etc.].

6. Play the Sarah Vaughan recording. At this point, students should be able to identify the style as jazz singing and explain why. Have students compare the two piano-accompanied recordings (Bennett and Vaughan) for piano style and also discuss the disparity in lengths of the two recordings. Note that classic Broadway show songs, especially from the thirties and forties, often became hit pop songs and later evolved into jazz standards. Ask students to discuss what they perceive to be the distinction between pop and jazz styles. Lead them to discover that improvisation is a major facet of jazz.

(continued)

- Students have some experience in aurally analyzing unfamiliar recordings.

7. Play several versions of another American standard song and ask students to identify the genre of each, based on what they have been learning about each genre.

Indicators of Success

- Students identify the genre (pop, jazz) of each version of a song.
- Students describe the historic relationship between Broadway show songs, American pop songs, and jazz standards.

Follow-up

- Ask students to name more current Broadway shows that have produced pop hits (e.g., *Cats*—"Memory"). Discuss with them the particular characteristics of many contemporary theatre songs that make them less suitable for adaptation as pop hits and especially jazz improvisation.

STANDARD 9C

Understanding music in relation to history and culture: Students identify various roles that musicians perform, cite representative individuals who have functioned in each role, and describe their activities and achievements.

Objective

- Students will describe the role of the master musician in traditional African performance practice and perform a similar role using an African song.

Materials

- "Wonfa Nyem," a mourning song from Ghana, in *Let Your Voice Be Heard: Songs from Ghana and Zimbabwe,* 2d ed., by Abraham Kobena Adzenyah, Dumisani Maraire, and Judith Cook Tucker (Danbury, CT: World Music Press, 1997), book and audiocassette

- African percussion instruments

- Audio-playback equipment

Prior Knowledge and Experiences

- Students have learned to sing "Wonfa Nyem" and they have used percussion instruments in rehearsing it.

- Students understand the meaning of the text of "Wonfa Nyem" and the context of the song.

- Students have had some experience with African instruments or body percussion.

- Students have improvised using the call-and-response form.

Procedures

1. Using Appendix A in *Let Your Voice Be Heard* as a guide, introduce students to the role of the master musician in African musical culture. Discuss with them the importance and function of this role in leading singing, drumming, and dancing.

2. Discuss with students the various aspects of the role of master musician and how best to perform them (e.g., the importance of clear signals, strong vocal lead, good eye contact, rhythmic accuracy).

3. Choose a student to be master musician and have the rest of the class sit in a circle. Tell the master musician to sing and speak the solo parts of "Wonfa Nyem" as the group sings the responses. Encourage the master musician to make eye contact with the entire group, in order to guide them vocally and visually. Tell students to think about the meaning of the text and to think of a possible scenario to put it in context. Encourage them to use their imaginations.

4. Invite different students to take on the role of master musician. As different students practice and become more comfortable in the role, encourage them to lead the group in percussion call-and-responses with African percussion instruments, clapping, and body percussion. Encourage students who are playing the role of master musician to push the limits of their imaginations and lead the group in ostinatos, improvisations based on call-and-response, and so on. Let the master musician control the entire piece from the slow opening section through the up-tempo section until the end.

Indicators of Success

- Students describe the characteristics of the role of master musician.

- Students demonstrate their understanding of the role of master musician, using appropriate eye contact and leading the group in ostinatos and call-and-response improvisations.

(continued)

Follow-up

- Have students explore the place of a master musician in other musical styles and cultures. Ask students to compare the role of master musician in traditional African performance practice with the role of the leader in a jazz combo, a rock band, a gospel choir, a madrigal group, and a symphony orchestra.

STANDARD 9C

Understanding music in relation to history and culture: Students identify various roles that musicians perform, cite representative individuals who have functioned in each role, and describe their activities and achievements.

Objective

- Students discover and describe biographical and cultural background information on a famous composer.

Materials

- Appropriate Mozart choral selection (see step 6)
- Students' "gifts for Mozart"
- Chalkboard

Other Requirements (optional)

- Actor (perhaps a friend who participates in community musical theater or opera productions) to play Mozart (or do it yourself)—see step 4

Prior Knowledge and Experiences

- Students have been rehearsing the selected Mozart work.

Procedures

1. Ask students to put their gifts for Mozart on a decorated table as they come into the classroom on the day of the party. Treat the rehearsal as a real birthday party (decorations, music of Mozart, cake, and so on).

2. Ask individual students to show their gifts to the class and relate their experiences digging into available resources. Have them describe how they creatively processed the information they uncovered. Ask how they narrowed down their choices. Be sure that each student gives the class some specific information he or she learned about Mozart's life and times. As this information unfolds, write it on the chalkboard and have students make notes in their journals.

3. Award prizes for the most unique, imaginative, or creative gifts.

4. Have "Mozart" make a costumed visit to share information about himself in a question-and-answer session. Add appropriate information to the list on the chalkboard.

5. Discuss with students the information on the chalkboard, helping them integrate the facts logically into a composite picture of Mozart. Give particular attention to Mozart's activities and achievements. Also, from facts on the board or other ideas students contribute, lead them in a discussion of the role of a musician in Mozart's time. Ask them what other musical roles Mozart had besides composer (e.g., performer).

6. Guide students to see any connections between the information they have learned and the style of the Mozart work they have been rehearsing. Have students sing the work in tribute to the "guest of honor."

Indicators of Success

- Students identify and describe Mozart's musical roles and accomplishments.

Follow-up

- Have students write a letter to Mozart, thanking him for his visit and highlighting the discoveries they made about him.

(continued)

- In preparation for a "Birthday Party for Mozart," perhaps on or near the anniversary of Mozart's birthday (January 27), students have been researching the life of Mozart in order to find a suitable gift. Students have been encouraged to use their imaginations to think of an appropriate gift, which they have brought to class on this day. The gifts could be anything at all, but students have been asked to choose gifts that would be logical for the "guest of honor." Students were not required to write reports, but they were asked to take notes in their journals as they researched biographical, historical, or cultural aspects of Mozart's life. They were encouraged to find out where he lived and when and to uncover details about Mozart's life and cultural milieu in order to come up with creative gift ideas.

Understanding music in relation to history and culture: Students identify and explain the stylistic features of a given musical work that serve to define its aesthetic tradition and its historical or cultural context.

Objective

- Students will demonstrate an understanding of musical style as a product of time and place, comparing two works of the same historical period but from different cultures.

Materials

- "David's Lamentation" by William Billings (Fort Lauderdale, FL: Walton Music Corporation), W2203, SATB, Level 2

- Recording of *Coronation Mass* by Wolfgang Amadeus Mozart

- Audio-playback equipment

- Chalkboard

Prior Knowledge and Experiences

- Students have rehearsed "David's Lamentation," and they understand how the piece is constructed.

- Students have studied the characteristics of music from various style periods.

- Students have studied the elements of music.

Procedures

1. Have students sing "David's Lamentation" all the way through as a review.

2. Tell students you are going to play a recording of another piece written at almost the same time as Billings wrote "David's Lamentation." Ask them to see if they can guess the composer or where the piece comes from. Play the recording of *Coronation Mass*.

3. Lead a discussion in which students speculate on the composer and style period of the recorded piece. Give them clues if necessary. When they have determined the composer and style period, ask them whether the two pieces actually sound like they were written at the same time. Have them explain their answers.

4. On the chalkboard, create two columns with the headings Billings and Mozart. Tell students that you are going to list all the aspects of the two pieces that they can name (e.g., characteristics of the melody, harmonies, accompaniment, dynamics, overall mood, size of forces) for a clear comparison of the two works. Lead them to discover the huge disparity between the two works in terms of style, especially the elegance, refinement, and relative sophistication of the Mozart work compared to the stark, much simpler, and more direct style of the Billings piece.

5. Ask students to speculate on why the styles of these two contemporaries are so different. Help them focus on time and place, aspects of each composer's social setting, level of education, intended audience, and purpose in writing. Fill in the missing information in their discussion. Eventually, students should see the Billings work as a reflection of the early American style—simple, direct, often untrained, but still highly effective—and the Mozart as a reflection of the European tradition.

6. Ask students what it is about "David's Lamentation" that is typically American and why or how the plainer, simpler, more direct style was the American style. Let students share their perceptions of Boston in the 1770s and the nature of art and music at the time. Help them to compare the music to what they may know of early American crafts, housewares, furniture, and architecture.

(continued)

Indicators of Success

- Students describe stylistic differences between Mozart and Billings, using appropriate vocabulary.

- Students explain Billings's style in relation to the time and place in which he composed.

Follow-up

- Ask students to discuss who they think is the "better" composer—Mozart or Billings—and why.

- Have students study the painting *Portrait of Paul Revere,* by John Copley, to discover its clear, sharp-edged, extremely realistic style and its direct focus and plain, informal, "everyday" feeling. Point out that Revere looks the observer straight in the eye while he pauses during his everyday silversmith work. Highlight the plain and direct style of this painting by a contemporary of Billings.

STANDARD 9D

Understanding music in relation to history and culture: Students identify and explain the stylistic features of a given musical work that serve to define its aesthetic tradition and its historical or cultural context.

Objective

- Students will identify and explain the cultural and historical context of a given song, discover its cultural meanings, and construct an interpretation that is meaningful for the ensemble.

Materials

- *Three Mountain Ballads,* arr. Ron Nelson (Bryn Mawr, PA: Theodore Presser Company), 36203075, SSA, Level 4
- Worksheets (see step 2)
- Audiotape of students singing "He's Gone Away"
- Audiocassette recorder

Prior Knowledge and Experiences

- Students have been rehearsing *Three Mountain Ballads* and have recorded their singing of the ballad "He's Gone Away."

Procedures

1. Play the recording of "He's Gone Away" and have students follow in their scores for *Three Mountain Ballads.* Ask students to describe their overall impressions of the piece in a class discussion.

2. Ask a student to read the words aloud. Then have students respond to the following questions from their worksheets:

   - Where has "he" gone? How does "she" feel?

   - Is there anything that makes you uncomfortable as you listen to the words?

   - In what historical period was this piece written? How were women treated then? (Consider things such as clothing; appropriate professions; reason for participating in music—to attract a man; role in marriage, economics, and so on.)

   - How does the music/accompaniment contribute to a sense of femininity? Stylistically, what kind of mood is the arranger creating and what instruments might he be imitating?

   - Have women's roles in society changed today? Does this song describe the experiences of any modern women? How is this piece an example of both an 1890s' cultural image of women and a modern cultural image of women?

   - What, if any, are good reasons for learning and performing this music?

   - If you could rewrite the text, what would you change?

3. When students have completed the worksheets, have them discuss their answers and the reasons for their answers. Guide them in recognizing the correct time period and in examining the specific features of the music that would lead them to that answer (e.g., the melodic lines; leading and then retreating from "tie," "glove," and "kiss" to emphasize the text).

4. Have students sing through "He's Gone Away."

Indicators of Success

- Students describe in writing their feelings and understanding of the piece.

(continued)

- Students identify the historical and cultural context of the piece.

Follow-up

- Ask students to bring in contemporary pop music that shares sentiments similar to those in "He's Gone Away." Discuss the cultural constructions of femininity in these songs and how they are similar to or different from "He's Gone Away."

- Point out to students that "He's Gone Away" is one of the most beloved pieces of the women's choir repertoire, but the image it projects of a woman may be jarring to contemporary sensibilities. Ask students to choose another piece in their choral repertoire and to write an essay discussing what that piece suggests to them about being a woman.

STANDARD 9E

Advanced

Understanding music in relation to history and culture: *Students identify and describe music genres or styles that show the influence of two or more cultural traditions, identify the cultural source of each influence, and trace the historical conditions that produced the synthesis of influences.*

Objective

- Students will identify and contrast the influences of rural European American culture and African American culture on performances of a spiritual.

Materials

- "Amazing Grace," arr. John Newton and Edward Lojeski (Milwaukee: Hal Leonard Corporation), 8300531, SATB, Level 1

- Video recording *Amazing Grace with Bill Moyers* (Princeton, NJ: Films for the Humanities and Sciences, 1990)

- Videocassette recorder

- Video monitor

- Chalkboard

Prior Knowledge and Experiences

- Students have been rehearsing "Amazing Grace."

Procedures

1. Show students excerpts from the video *Amazing Grace with Bill Moyers* that feature the African-American Wiregrass Singers and the Sacred Harp Singers.

2. Discuss with students the differences they hear in the two groups' versions of "Amazing Grace." Have students discuss characteristics of the two different styles and contrast them as you list them on the chalkboard. If necessary, play the video excerpts more than once.

3. Point out to students the characteristics that are specific to the African American tradition and those that are specific to the European American tradition.

4. Ask students to identify whether the style of the "Amazing Grace" arrangement they have been rehearsing is in the African American or European American tradition [European American]. Discuss the stylistic features they observed in the video that they can apply to their own music.

5. Have students sing through "Amazing Grace."

Indicators of Success

- Students identify the characteristics of African American and European American performances of spirituals and describe the influence of the cultural traditions on each performance.

- Students perform "Amazing Grace" in the proper style of the publication.

Follow-up

- Show students the entire video of *Amazing Grace with Bill Moyers*. Discuss with them the background of the song and help them to consider the influence of the lifestyles and socioeconomic conditions of these two cultures on their music-making traditions.

RESOURCES

Choral Music Referenced in This Text

"Adieu, Ye City-Prisoning Towers" by Thomas Tomkins. SSATB. Level 3. In *Oxford Book of English Madrigals,* edited by Philip Ledger. New York: Oxford University Press, 1979.

P. 34 "Agnus Dei" by Samuel Barber. Milwaukee: Hal Leonard Corporation. HL50313910. SATB. Level 6.

"Agnus Dei," from *Missa Dixit Maria,* by Hans Leo Hassler. Miami: Warner Bros. Publications. SV9007. SATB. Level 3.

P. 22 + 99 "Amazing Grace," arr. John Newton and Edward Lojeski. Milwaukee: Hal Leonard Corporation. 8300531. SATB. Level 1.

P. 41 "April Is in My Mistress' Face" by Thomas Morley. Boston: E. C. Schirmer. 1612. SATB. Level 3.

"Ca' the Yowes," arr. Mary Goetze. New York: Boosey & Hawkes. 6258. SA. Level 3.

P. 55 "Choose Something Like a Star," from *Frostiana,* by Randall Thompson. Boston: E. C. Schirmer. 2487. SATB. Level 5.

"Crucifixus," from Mass in B minor, by Johann Sebastian Bach. Milwaukee: Hal Leonard Corporation. 08678813. SATB. Level 4.

P. 60 + 95 "David's Lamentation" by William Billings. Fort Lauderdale, FL: Walton Music Corporation. W2203. SATB. Level 2.

P. 16 "David's Lamentation" by G. S. Wilson. Milwaukee: G. Schirmer/Hal Leonard Corporation. 50312130. SATB. Level 3.

"Dixit Maria," from *Missa Dixit Maria,* by Hans Leo Hassler. Miami: Warner Bros. Publications. FEC 09679. SATB. Level 3.

"Epitaph for Moonlight" by R. Murray Schafer. Toronto: Berandol Music. BER1094. SSSSAAAATTTTBBBB. Level 5.

P. 18 "Fair Phyllis I Saw Sitting All Alone" by John Farmer. Fort Lauderdale, FL: Walton Music Corporation. W8000. SATB. Level 3.

"For unto Us a Child Is Born," from *Messiah,* by George Frideric Handel. New York: Carl Fischer. 50294190. SATB. Level 5.

"Hallelujah Chorus," from *Messiah,* by George Frideric Handel. New York: Carl Fischer. CM86. SATB. Level 5.

"I Love My Love," Cornish folk song, arr. Gustav Holst. New York: G. Schirmer/Hal Leonard Corporation. 5029920. SATB. Level 5.

"Jesus Said to the Blind Man" by Melchior Vulpius, arr. Hans Eggebrecht. St. Louis: Concordia Publishing House. 981027. SATB. Level 5.

P. 29 "Meine Tage in dem Leide," from Cantata 150, by Johann Sebastian Bach. Miami: Warner Bros. Publications. K06056. SATB. Level 3–4.

P. 32 "Miniwanka" by R. Murray Schafer. Indian River, Ontario, Canada: Arcana Editions. Treble voices alone or SATB. Level 2.

P. 7 "Now Is the Month of Maying" by Thomas Morley. Boston: E. C. Schirmer. 1155. SATB. Level 4.

P. 72 "Peaceful Vale" ("Ruhetal" or "Valley of Rest") by Felix Mendelssohn, arr. Frank Mueller. Van Nuys, CA: Alfred Publishing Company. 04-70603. SATB. Level 3.

P. 58 "Resonet in Laudibus" by Chester L. Alwes. Dayton, OH: The Lorenz Corporation. 10/1264R. SATB. Level 3.

"Resonet in Laudibus" by Jacob Handl. Fort Lauderdale, FL: Walton Music Corporation. W2151. SATB. Level 2.

"Resonet in Laudibus" by Z. Randall Stroope. Champaign, IL: Mark Foster Music. MF553. SATB. Level 3.

P. 76 "Sakura," arr. Linda Steen Spevacek. Milwaukee: Hal Leonard Corporation. 08756912. Two-part. Level 3.

"Shenandoah," arr. James Erb. New York: Lawson-Gould Music Publishers/Alfred Publishing Company. 04-51846. SSAATTBB. Level 3.

"Shenandoah," arr. Mary Goetze. New York: Boosey & Hawkes. OCTB6257. SSA. Level 3.

"Sicut Cervus" by Giovanni Pierluigi Palestrina. Any standard edition. Level 4.

"Sicut Locutus Est," from *Magnificat,* by Johann Sebastian Bach. New York: Carl Fischer. CM8111. SSATB. Level 4.

P. 80 "Sunday," from *Sunday in the Park with George,* by Stephen Sondheim. Miami: Warner Bros. Publications. VAL2018. Vocal selections.

P. 54 "Take, O Take Those Lips Away," from *Three Madrigals,* by Emma Lou Diemer. New York: Boosey & Hawkes. OCTB5417. SATB. Level 3.

p. 97 *(handwritten)*

Three Mountain Ballads, arr. by Ron Nelson. Bryn Mawr, PA: Theodore Presser Company. 36203075. SSA. Level 4.

p. 39 *(handwritten)*

"The Turtle Dove," arr. Linda Steen Spevacek. Milwaukee: Jenson/Hal Leonard Corporation. 43725024. SATB with flute. Level 3.

p. 15 *(handwritten)*

"Valiant for Truth" by Ralph Vaughan Williams. New York: Oxford University Press. 0-19353-529-7. SATB. Level 5.

18 octavos *(handwritten)*

"We Shall Not Give Up the Fight," from *Freedom Is Coming: Songs of Protest and Praise from South Africa,* by Anders Nyberg, edited by Henry H. Leck. Fort Lauderdale, FL: Walton Music Corporation. WW1149, three-part, Level 2; WW1174, SAB, Level 2.

"When David Heard" by Norman Dinerstein. New York: Boosey & Hawkes. BH 6014. SATB. Level 5.

"When David Heard" by Thomas Weelkes. New York: Oxford University Press. 0-19352-211-X. SATB. Level 5.

Books Referenced in This Text

Adzenyah, Abraham Kobena, Dumisani Maraire, and Judith Cook Tucker. *Let Your Voice Be Heard: Songs from Ghana and Zimbabwe,* 2d ed. Danbury, CT: World Music Press, 1997. Book and audiocassette.

*Anderson, William A., and Patricia Shehan Campbell, eds. *Multicultural Perspectives in Music Education,* 2d ed. Reston, VA: Music Educators National Conference, 1996.

Chapman, Anne, ed. *Making Sense: Teaching Critical Reading Across the Curriculum.* New York: College Entrance Examination Board, 1993.

Fowler, Charles. *Music! Its Role and Importance in Our Lives.* New York: Glencoe/McGraw-Hill, 1994. Book and recordings.

Ledger, Philip, ed. *Oxford Book of English Madrigals.* New York: Oxford University Press, 1979.

Recordings Referenced in This Text

Aebersold, Jamey. *Jazz: How to Play and Improvise,* vol. 1. Jamey Aebersold Jazz, PO Box 1244C, New Albany, IN 47151.

The American Popular Song Collection, disc 5. Smithsonian CD RP0006.

Art of the Koto: The Music of Japan Played by Kimia Eto. Elektra Records CD 70234.

Black Angels. Kronos Quartet. Elektra Nonesuch CD9 79242-2.

A Cathedral Concert. Bulgarian State Radio and Television Female Choir. Verve World 314-510794-2.

Jazz Sebastian Bach. The Swingle Singers. Philips 824-703-2.

Out of This World. Chanticleer. Joseph Jennings. Teldec 4509-96515-2.

The Rodgers & Hart Songbook, vol. 2. Verve 821579-2.

Schafer, R. Murray. *A Garden of Bells: Choral Music of R. Murray Schafer.* Vancouver Chamber Choir. Jon Washburn. Grouse Records 101 (Arcana Editions, Box 425, Station K, Toronto, ON, Canada M4P 2G9).

The Smithsonian Collection of Classic Jazz, disc 4. Smithsonian RJ0010.

Sondheim, Stephen. *Sunday in the Park with George.* RCA RCD1-5042.

The Swingle Singers: A Cappella Amadeus. The Swingle Singers. Virgin Classics Limited CD 0777 75961720.

Videotapes Referenced in This Text

Amazing Grace with Bill Moyers. Princeton, NJ: Films for the Humanities and Sciences, 1990.

Broadway Backstage! The Midtown Management Group, Inc., 120 West 44th Street, Suite 601, New York, NY 10036; telephone 212-398-6740. 1985.

Ferris Bueller's Day Off. Hollywood: Paramount Home Video, 1996.

Additional Resources

*Anderson, Tom. *Sing Choral Music at Sight.* Reston, VA: Music Educators National Conference, 1992.

Benward, Bruce, and Maureen A. Carr. *Sightsinging Complete,* 5th ed. Madison, WI: Brown & Benchmark/McGraw-Hill, 1991.

Bernstein, Leonard. *Young People's Concerts.* East Hartford: The Amberson Groups, 1994. Videocassettes and study guide.

DeCesare, Ruth. *Myth, Music and Dance of the American Indian.* Edited by Sandy Feldstein et al. Van Nuys, CA: Alfred Publishing Company, 1988.

Gabrieli, Giovanni. *The Glory of Venice—Gabrieli in San Marco.* CBS Records MK 42645. Compact disc.

———. *The Glory of Venice: Giovanni Gabrieli.* ARGO 417 468-2. Compact disc.

George, Luvenia A. *Teaching the Music of Six Different Cultures,* rev. ed. Danbury, CT: World Music Press, 1988. Book and audiocassette.

Herman, Sally. *In Search of Musical Excellence: Taking Advantage of Varied Learning Styles.* Dayton, OH: Lorenz Corporation, 1993.

Janson, H. W., and Anthony F. Janson. *History of Art for Young People,* 5th ed. New York: Harry N. Abrams, 1997.

Jeffers, Ron, comp. *Translations and Annotations of Choral Repertoire.* Vol. 1, *Sacred Latin Texts.* Corvallis, OR: Earthsongs, 1988.

*Jordanoff, Christine, and Robert Page. *Choral Triad Video Workshop.* QED Communications. Reston, VA: Music Educators National Conference, 1994. Six-videocassette series and workbook.

King's Singers, The. *The King's Singers' Madrigal History Tour.* EMI CDM 7 69837 2. Compact disc.

Lomax, Alan. *North American Folksongs.* London: Cassels, 1960.

May, Will V., ed. *Something New to Sing About,* Level 2. Mission Hills, CA: Glencoe/McGraw-Hill, 1989.

*May, William V., and Craig Tolin. *Pronunciation Guide for Choral Literature.* Reston, VA: Music Educators National Conference. 1987.

McCalla, James. *Jazz: A Listener's Guide.* Englewood Cliffs, NJ: Prentice-Hall, 1982.

Megill, Donald D., and Richard S. Demory. *Introduction to Jazz History,* 4th ed. Englewood Cliffs, NJ: Prentice-Hall, 1995.

Mittler, Gene A. *Art in Focus: Aesthetics, Criticism, History, Studio,* 3d ed. New York: Glencoe/McGraw-Hill, 1993.

*Music Educators National Conference. *Teaching Choral Music: A Course of Study.* Reston, VA: Author, 1991.

Rao, Doreen. *We Will Sing!* New York: Boosey & Hawkes, 1993.

Rodgers, Richard, and Lorenz Hart. *Babes in Arms.* Produced by Arthur Freed. Library Video Company, PO Box 580, Wynnewood, PA 19096; telephone 800-843-3620. Videocassette.

Sandburg, Carl. *The American Songbag.* Orlando, FL: Harcourt Brace, 1990.

Southern, Eileen. *The Music of Black Americans: A History,* 3d ed. New York: W. W. Norton, 1997.

Swafford, Jan. *The Vintage Guide to Classical Music.* New York: Vintage/Random House, 1993.

Walsh, Michael. *Who's Afraid of Classical Music?* New York: Fireside/Simon & Schuster Trade, 1989.

Whitlock, Ruth. *Choral Insights.* 4 vols. San Diego: Neil A. Kjos Music Company.

Wold, Milo, Gary Martin, James Miller, and Edmund Cykler. *An Outline History of Western Music,* 7th ed. Dubuque: Madison, WI: Brown & Benchmark/McGraw-Hill, 1989.

---

*Available from MENC.

MENC Resources on Music and Arts Education Standards

Aiming for Excellence: The Impact of the Standards Movement on Music Education. 1996. #1012.

Implementing the Arts Education Standards. Set of five brochures: "What School Boards Can Do," "What School Administrators Can Do," "What State Education Agencies Can Do," "What Parents Can Do," "What the Arts Community Can Do." 1994. #4022. Each brochure is also available in packs of 20.

Music for a Sound Education: A Tool Kit for Implementing the Standards. 1994. #1600.

National Standards for Arts Education: What Every Young American Should Know and Be Able to Do in the Arts. 1994. #1605.

Opportunity-to-Learn Standards for Music Instruction: Grades PreK–12. 1994. #1619.

Performance Standards for Music: Strategies and Benchmarks for Assessing Progress Toward the National Standards, Grades PreK–12. 1996. #1633.

Perspectives on Implementation: Arts Education Standards for America's Students. 1994. #1622.

"Prekindergarten Music Education Standards" (brochure). 1995. #4015 (set of 10).

The School Music Program—A New Vision: The K–12 National Standards, PreK Standards, and What They Mean to Music Educators. 1994. #1618.

"Teacher Education in the Arts Disciplines: Issues Raised by the National Standards for Arts Education." 1996. #1609.

Teaching Examples: Ideas for Music Educators. 1994. #1620.

The Vision for Arts Education in the 21st Century. 1994. #1617.

MENC's *Strategies for Teaching* Series

Strategies for Teaching Prekindergarten Music, compiled and edited by Wendy L. Sims. #1644.

Strategies for Teaching K–4 General Music, compiled and edited by Sandra L. Stauffer and Jennifer Davidson. #1645.

Strategies for Teaching Middle-Level General Music, compiled and edited by June M. Hinckley and Suzanne M. Shull. #1646.

Strategies for Teaching High School General Music, compiled and edited by Keith P. Thompson and Gloria J. Kiester. #1647.

Strategies for Teaching Elementary and Middle-Level Chorus, compiled and edited by Ann Roberts Small and Judy K. Bowers. #1648.

Strategies for Teaching High School Chorus, compiled and edited by Randal Swiggum. #1649.

Strategies for Teaching Strings and Orchestra, compiled and edited by Dorothy A. Straub, Louis S. Bergonzi, and Anne C. Witt. #1652.

Strategies for Teaching Middle-Level and High School Keyboard, compiled and edited by Martha F. Hilley and Tommie Pardue. #1655.

Strategies for Teaching Beginning and Intermediate Band, compiled and edited by Edward J. Kvet and Janet M. Tweed. #1650.

Strategies for Teaching High School Band, compiled and edited by Edward J. Kvet and John E. Williamson. #1651.

Strategies for Teaching Specialized Ensembles, compiled and edited by Robert A. Cutietta. #1653.

Strategies for Teaching Middle-Level and High School Guitar, compiled and edited by William E. Purse, James L. Jordan, and Nancy Marsters. #1654.

Strategies for Teaching: Guide for Music Methods Classes, compiled and edited by Louis O. Hall with Nancy R. Boone, John Grashel, and Rosemary C. Watkins. #1656.

For more information on these and other MENC publications, write to or call MENC Publications Sales, 1806 Robert Fulton Drive, Reston, VA 20191-4348; 800-828-0229.